THE TOP 100
TRADITIONAL
REMEDIES

THE TOP 100 TRADITIONAL REMEDIES

SARAH MERSON

INDEX

The Top 100 Traditional Remedies
Sarah Merson

First published in the United Kingdom and Ireland in 2007 by
Duncan Baird Publishers Ltd
Sixth Floor, Castle House
75–76 Wells Street, London W1T 3QH

Conceived, created and designed by
Duncan Baird Publishers

This edition published 2007 for Index Books Ltd

Managing Editor: Grace Cheetham
Editor: Krystyna Mayer
Managing Designer: Manisha Patel
Designer: Gail Jones
Commissioned photography: Simon Smith and Toby Scott

British Library Cataloguing-in-Publication Data:
A CIP record for this book is available from the British Library

ISBN: 978-1-84483-555-3

10 9 8 7 6 5 4 3 2 1

Typeset in Helvetica Condensed
Colour reproduction by Colourscan, Singapore
Printed in Thailand by Imago

Publisher's Note: The information in this book is not intended as a substitute for professional medical treatment and advice. The publishers and author cannot accept responsibility for any damage incurred as a result of any of the therapeutic methods contained in this work. The therapeutic methods contained in this book are intended for adult use only. It is advisable to consult a medical professional before using any of these methods, particularly if you are pregnant, breastfeeding or suffering from a medical condition and are unsure of the suitability of any of the remedies or foods mentioned in this book. All recipes serve four unless specified otherwise.

CONTENTS

KEY

- anti-allergenic
- antibacterial
- anti-inflammatory
- anti-viral
- antioxidant
- antiseptic
- detoxifying
- good for the heart
- good for the skin
- helps the digestive system
- immunity boosting

traditional remedies

"Health is the expression of a harmonious balance between various components of man's nature, the environment and ways of life…nature is the physician of disease."

HIPPPOCRATES

Traditional home remedies offer safe health treatments that have been passed down through the generations. Moreover, they can be prepared at home using plants, foods and other readily available ingredients.

In a quest to bring natural ingredients and health back into our lives, we are incorporating traditional home remedies with ever more vigour. Not only can such remedies offer tried and tested solutions to many symptoms, but they may also help us to prevent the development of ill-health in the first place.

Dating back to before ancient Egyptian times, remedies steeped in mythological and spiritual beliefs were once used as part of everyday life. They have naturally evolved over time, and have had an eventful history. The great physicians of ancient Greece – Hippocrates, Galen, Theophrastus and Dioscorides – drew on the Egyptian culture when writing their own works. Their texts were kept alive through the Dark Ages in Europe, copied by successive generations of Christian monks, and given a new lease of life with the discovery of printing in the mid-15th century. European scholars then documented and illustrated a wide variety of foods and plants, along with accounts of their remedial and hallucinatory properties, soporific and stimulating effects, and other qualities. In the 16th century European physicians such as John Gerard and Nicholas Culpeper took on a new line of work, based on the empirical observations of plants. In some cases herbal remedies began to be used in conjunction with general medicine. However, in the 1800s conventional medicine began seeking to establish a monopoly, and in a number of Western countries legislation was imposed. This banned the practice of medicine by anyone who had not been trained in a conventional medical school. Scepticism gradually set in and the medical establishment began concentrating entirely on laboratory-produced pharmaceuticals. Meanwhile, ancient remedies were deemed to be the work of mythical folklore and even witches. However, despite this resistance to them, natural remedies continued to prove their efficacy and this led to the formation of the National Institute of Medical Herbalists in 1864 – the first professional body of herbal practitioners in the world. Due to organizations such as this, traditional remedies have been afforded much of the learned wisdom of the past, as well as the benefits of modern discoveries.

For example, the ancient idea that everyday food has distinct pharmacological properties that can be used to promote health may at first seem like folklore that is decidedly deficient in the rigorous scientific proof required in the 21st century. But today,

ANCIENT MEDICINAL REMEDIES

- The ancient Egyptians were the first to use a method known as "infusion" to extract the oils from aromatic plants.
- The early Aztecs used garlic to prevent tuberculosis.
- The Romans cured hiccups by consuming small amounts of raw cabbage in vinegar.
- The Romans took much of their medical knowledge from the Greeks, and then refined the use of many remedies.
- During the building of the pyramids, Egyptian workers were given garlic daily to rid them of spirits and give them the vitality and strength to perform well.
- It was a Roman tradition to use the yolks of eggs, mixed with the ash of their shells, for dysentery.
- The Aztecs once smeared avocado pulp on sexual organs to enhance sexual appetite.
- The Egyptians mixed together the fats of lion, hippo, cat, crocodile and serpent to anoint the head of a bald person and stimulate hair growth.

authoritative research into natural healing is progressing at a rapid pace, and traditional plant lore has proven itself with evidence of its medicinal properties. This evolution has even been encouraged by the scientific community, which is inceasingly recognizing the numerous benefits of plants and other natural substances through experimentation and experience.

THE USE OF NATURAL THERAPEUTICS IN A CHANGING WORLD

There exists a real alchemy with the majority of ingredients used in traditional remedies.

For example, plants take from the soil essential nutritive substances that they then store and convert into usable forms. They are, therefore, natural reservoirs of precious elements drawn from the soil, which past generations have had the wisdom and down-to-earth common sense to make good use of. Unfortunately, since the Industrial Revolution many of the soils in developed countries have changed dramatically. This, in turn, has led to a decline in the quality of our food.

In order to get the best from nature's garden, we need to be reminded of the practices our ancestors observed:

NATUROPATHIC GUIDELINES FOR BETTER HEALTH

- Lead a wholesome lifestyle.
- Eat organic, unadulterated food.
- Eat local, seasonal produce whenever possible.
- Eat slowly, chewing food thoroughly.
- Avoid processed and junk food.
- Drink 2 litres (3½ pints/8 cups) of pure, clean water each day.
- Try to detox your body twice a year.
- Wear clothing made from natural fibres and dyes.
- Choose skin-care products free of chemicals, foaming agents, and so on.
- Always use natural deodorants rather than chemical anti-perspirants.
- Make sure you get plenty of sunlight.
- Stimulate circulation and excretion of toxins through daily skin brushing.
- Get plenty of rest and relaxation to maintain your body's inherent healing mechanisms.
- Exercise for at least 30 minutes 3–4 times a week – walking, yoga, Pilates and tai chi are all examples of good types of exercise.
- Try to achieve a healthy life balance: take time out to relax in the company of your family and friends.

• Look to Mother Nature – remember plants growing in the wild are a product of nature and therefore have more innately potent properties than those of modern cultivated varieties.

• When selecting plants it is preferable to choose from those that are growing some distance apart, rather than those tightly packed together.

• Always choose fruits, vegetables and herbs that have the most fragrance, taste and colour. These are the ones that are also the most fresh and nutritive.

TOWARDS SELF-HEALING

It may no longer be necessary for us to go foraging in the woods and hedgerows, or to hunt wild animals as our ancestors did. Today, many ingredients that were hunted and gathered by our forefathers are commonly available in health-food stores and even supermarkets, and they can do much to help us live healthy lives.

We know that many natural ingredients have proven medicinal value, as well as providing sustenance, yet the dividing line between "food" and "medicine" is not always clear. However, we have learned that when it comes to healing, they are, in fact, part of the same thing. Moreover, such is the way of traditional remedies that – whether they are ingested internally or used topically – the body will take what it needs from the food or plant with the ultimate goal of rebalancing the system. This union with nature ultimately allows us to regain our own innate ability to heal ourselves.

While our lifestyles are very different from those of our ancestors, traditional remedies – which are innately nurturing and healing – can have huge benefits on our current hurried lifestyles, and we need them more today than we have ever done.

This book provides details of some of the most important properties of 100 of the best natural ingredients that can be used to maintain and often improve health. Symbols supplementing the text give at-a-glance information on the key properties of each ingredient described.

The use of traditional remedies places every aspect of health back in our own hands and leaves little doubt that it is worth rediscovering our roots.

lemon

Used originally by the Romans to sweeten the breath, lemons are packed full of nutrients and are used today to treat a number of ailments.

Lemons are rich in citrus flavonoids such as vitamin C, and have important antioxidant functions. They can strengthen the immune system, assist the healing of wounds and strengthen the walls of blood capillaries. Because of their antiseptic qualities, lemons are used to treat infections of the respiratory tract. Their dissolving and extracting qualities help in the topical treatment of boils and abscesses. Lemons are also a liver stimulant, and can therefore be used for detoxification – for example, when drank as lemon water.

PROPERTIES/ACTIONS
- Strengthening
- Extracting
- Boosts immunity
- Liver stimulant

PARTS USED
- Whole fruit

LEMON POULTICE
for boils & abscesses

1 lemon, sliced
gauze bandage

Use the bandage to tie a slice of lemon against the boil or abscess. A hot-water bottle can be used to apply heat, if desired. Leave for about 10 minutes, then discard. Repeat 2 or 3 times a day until the boil opens and drains.

orange

Native to tropical Asia, oranges are a wholesome food, high in vitamin C and fibre and rich in natural sugars for quick energy.

Oranges are a top source of vitamin C. They are great immune boosters and have a reputation for fighting against colds. Oranges contain various other antioxidants, which together help temper high cholesterol, reduce inflammation, and block cancer cells. They are high in fibre, helping to relieve many intestinal problems, and are great energizers.

Healing neroli oil from orange tree leaves has been used for thousands of years.

PROPERTIES/ACTIONS
• Boosts immunity
• Lowers cholesterol
• Energizing

PARTS USED
• Whole fruit

ORANGE SHERBET

750ml (24fl oz/3 cups) fresh orange juice
55g (2oz/¼ cup) raw sugar
2 tbsp milk
½ tsp vanilla essence
125ml (4fl oz/½ cup) water

Combine the ingredients. Pour into a tray and place in the freezer. Once frozen, cut into strips and blend in a food processor. Serve at once.

apricot

As their bright orange colour shows, apricots are rich in beta-carotene. They have been prominent in Indian and Chinese folklore for 2,000 years.

Apricots have high levels of beta-carotene, which the body turns into anti-viral vitamin A. Eating fresh apricots can be helpful to those suffering from infection, particularly infections of the respiratory tract. Dried apricots supply iron and produce haemoglobin, which is beneficial to those suffering from anaemia. They also have a balancing effect on the nervous system, treating mental fatigue, mild anxiety and insomnia, and yield an oil that is highly nourishing and protective to the skin.

PROPERTIES/ACTIONS
- Balancing
- Supports respiratory tract
- Rich in iron

PARTS USED
- Whole fruit

APRICOT MASSAGE OIL
for dry, sensitive skins

250g (9oz) apricot seeds
750ml (26fl oz/3 cups)
carrier oil
piece of muslin

With a pestle and mortar, grind the seeds to release the oils, then place them in a clear glass jar. Pour the carrier oil onto the seeds, secure and shake. Place in a sunny spot and leave for 2 to 6 weeks. Pour the oil through a muslin-lined sieve into a jug, then pour into dark glass bottles. Store for up to a year. Apply liberally to the skin when needed.

fig

Nature's own laxative, figs are indigenous to Persia, Syria and other parts of Asia, and are generously high in healthful compounds.

Figs contain active ingredients that stimulate the intestinal action needed for bowel movement. They are also a rich source of soluble fibre, which has a laxative effect.

Figs contain good amounts of potassium, a mineral that is essential for keeping blood pressure down. Being rich in iron, they are excellent for pregnant women and convalescents. Used topically, they are good at drawing out poisons.

Spartan athletes in ancient Greece were said to eat figs to boost their performance.

PROPERTIES/ACTIONS
- Laxative
- High in fibre
- Rich in potassium

PARTS USED
- Whole fruit

FIG SYRUP
for constipation

50g (2oz/⅓ cup) dried figs
50g (2oz/⅓ cup) prunes
455ml (1 pint/16fl oz/2 cups) water
1 tbsp treacle

Put the water, figs and prunes in a saucepan. Soak for 8 hours, then bring to the boil and simmer until the fruit is soft and the excess liquid has reduced. Stir in the treacle, then cool and whizz in a food processor. Transfer to a jam jar and store in the refrigerator. Take 1 dessertspoon of the syrup as needed.

pineapple

Inside their tough skins, fresh pineapples have "hearts of gold": they are rich in bromelain, vitamin C and manganese.

PROPERTIES/ACTIONS
- Reduces inflammation
- Speeds tissue repair
- Protects bones
- Energizing

PARTS USED
- Whole fruit

Containing the enzyme bromelain, pineapple has a centuries-old reputation for its anti-inflammatory action. It is useful in treating conditions from sinusitis and rheumatoid arthritis, to sore throats and gout. It may help speed recovery from injuries and surgery, help alleviate fluid retention, and prevent blood clots and conditions such as arteriosclerosis. Bromelain can help the gut to operate efficiently and effectively, and is therefore a useful remedy for digestive problems. The vitamin C content in pineapples helps to thwart free radicals and

PINEAPPLE PEEL REMEDY
for dry, dead skin

**1 small, fresh pineapple
first-aid tape or light bandage
bowl of warm water**

Soak the dry skin area in water for 20 minutes. Cut a piece of pineapple peel and place it flesh side-down directly on the skin. Secure the peel with tape and leave overnight. Carefully remove the dressing, then soak the skin in water for 5 minutes. Repeat for approximately 4 consecutive nights.

PINEAPPLE & HONEY MARINADE   *for salmon or chicken*

**200g (7oz) fresh pineapple,
   peeled and finely chopped
2 garlic cloves, crushed
1–2 tbsp honey
1 tsp allspice
1 tsp freshly ground nutmeg
1 tsp ground cinnamon
1 tsp ground cloves**

pinch of salt

Mix together all the ingredients and leave to stand for 15 minutes. Pour over the salmon or chicken and leave to marinade for 2 hours, before cooking.

boost immunity. Vitamin C also helps to make bone-protecting collagen, and pineapples are a good source of manganese, which also makes collagen. Used topically, the bromelian content of pineapple can help to soften dead skin.

In ancient Indian medicine pineapples were thought to act as a uterine tonic.

raspberry

Raspberries are high in antioxidants and other protective nutrients essential for good health, and are commonly used as a home remedy.

This tart fruit contains a host of absorbable nutrients, from vitamin C to calcium, potassium, iron and magnesium, all of which are essential to the convalescent, as well as to those suffering from heart problems, fatigue and depression.

Raspberries are naturally astringent and can therefore help to treat upset stomachs and diarrhoea. An infusion made of raspberry leaves can facilitate labour by acting as both a uterine relaxant and a tonic.

PROPERTIES/ACTIONS
- Astringent
- Treats diarrhoea
- Uterine relaxant

PARTS USED
- Whole fruit & leaves

According to folklore raspberries have the ability to soothe inflamed tonsils.

RASPBERRY LEAF TEA *for painful periods or to facilitate labour*

60g (2¼oz/4 cups) fresh young raspberry leaves, or 25g (1oz/2 cups) dried leaves 500ml (16fl oz/2 cups) water, freshly boiled	Put the leaves in a large cup and pour over boiling water. Cover and leave to stand for 15 minutes, then strain. Drink up to 5 cups a day. Caution: use only from week 32 of pregnancy.

strawberry

Strawberries enhance liver and gallbladder functions, and are a traditional remedy for treating gout, arthritis and kidney stones.

Extremely high in antioxidants, strawberries contain ellagic acid, which is believed to help cellular changes leading to cancer. They are a good source of vitamin C, and can thus help to fight infection and heart disease.

The Romans used strawberries to relieve everything from loose teeth to gastritis.

Their high iron content makes them therapeutic for anaemia and fatigue. Strawberries are a mild laxative and antibacterial, and may help to regenerate intestinal flora. They can also dissolve tartarous incrustations on the teeth.

PROPERTIES/ACTIONS
- Astringent
- Diuretic
- Nervine

PARTS USED
- Whole fruit & leaves

STRAWBERRY & HONEY DECOCTION *for sore throats*

30g (1oz/⅙ cup) fresh strawberries
30g (1oz/1 cup) strawberry leaves
750ml (26fl oz/3 cups) water
honey, to taste

Place all the ingredients, except the honey, in an aluminium or a stainless steel pan. Bring to the boil and simmer, uncovered, for about 15 minutes to reduce. Add the honey. Strain and discard the ingredients. Transfer to a glass bottle with a lid and store in the refrigerator. Gargle 150ml of the mixture every 30 minutes.

grapefruit

Originating in Jamaica in 1814, grapefruit shares with other citrus fruits a high level of vitamin C and plenty of potassium.

HONEY-MARINATED GRAPEFRUIT

4 ruby grapefruit
2 tbsp honey
1 tbsp minced fresh mint

Squeeze the juice of 1 grapefruit and grate 1 teaspoon of the zest; set aside. Warm the honey in a saucepan. Add the juice and zest. Mix well. Peel the 3 grapefruit and separate into sections. Arrange on a plate and cover with the marinade. Leave to stand for 15 minutes. Sprinkle with mint.

The high vitamin-C content of grapefruit enhances immunity, helping to reduce and relieve colds, heal cuts and reduce bruising. Grapefruit is a potent source of pectin, and can therefore lower cholesterol and aid circulatory or digestive problems. The pinkish hue of grapefruit is due to the presence of lycopene, a powerful antioxidant that helps to protect against heart disease and cancer. Grapefruit also helps treat fungal infections.

Red grapefruit has a higher lycopene content than the white varieties.

apple

Over the course of centuries, apple has acquired a reputation as a healthful fruit and remedy, thus confirming the old adage, "An apple a day keeps the doctor away."

Stimulating the liver and kidneys, apples have a detoxifying effect on the body. They are rich in pectin, which binds to and helps dispel toxins and cholesterol, and malic acid, which neutralizes acid by-products. Apples may treat constipation and diarrhoea. They slow the rise of blood sugar and help control diabetes. Containing quercetin, an anti-inflammatory, apples lower the risk of heart disease and are useful in the treatment of arthritis and allergic reactions.

PROPERTIES/ACTIONS
• Dispels toxins
• Controls blood sugar
• Anti-inflammatory

PARTS USED
• Whole fruit

In Greek mythology, golden versions of apple grew on trees guarded by the Hesperides.

AGE-OLD APPLE & LIQUORICE INFUSION
for gastric, kidney & pulmonary conditions

2–3kg (4½–6½lb) apples, unpeeled and thinly sliced into rounds
1 litre (35fl oz/4 cups) water
2 small pieces liquorice root

Place the apples in a saucepan and cover with the water. Add the liquorice root and boil for 15 minutes, then strain and discard the apple and liquorice. Drink throughout the day.

cranberry

Due to their antibacterial properties, cranberries have become a renowned remedy for treating infections of the urinary tract and kidney stones.

PROPERTIES/ACTIONS
- Supports urinary tract
- Fights infection

PARTS USED
- Whole fruit

Cranberries are a valuable source of vitamin C, and the Native Americans first introduced Europeans to cranberries to help combat scurvy. It became recognized that the acidity of cranberries increases the natural acidity of urine, thus preventing bacteria from thriving. Cranberries are therefore very effective against cystitis. Being rich in antioxidants, cranberries may also help to ward off colds and other diseases, including some cancers.

CRANBERRY-ORANGE RELISH

300g (12oz/2 cups) cranberries, fresh or frozen
1 medium orange, unpeeled, cut into eighths and seeded
1 apple, unpeeled, cut into eighths and cored
75g (2½oz/⅓ cup) granulated sugar
1 tsp ground ginger

Blend the fruit in a food processor. Stir in the sugar and ginger, and transfer to a glass jar. Cover with a lid and refrigerate for at least 4 hours. Use when needed.

blueberry

An historical resource for herbalists and physicians, this scented fruit inhibits "unfriendly" bacteria to keep the gut clean and healthy.

Blueberries contain therapeutic agents lethal to bacteria, namely *E.coli,* and are a common folk remedy for urinary tract infections as well as diarrhoea. The tannins contained in the fruit are said to kill microbes.

As well as improving micro-circulation, blueberries contain high levels of antioxidants, which are believed to protect against heart disease, stroke, cancer and gum disease, and to enhance eyesight. They also treat coughs and colds.

PROPERTIES/ACTIONS
- Treats diarrhoea
- Fights infection
- Supports digestion

PARTS USED
- Whole fruit & leaves

Pilots on night missions have reported better vision after eating blueberry jam.

BLUEBERRY TEA
for coughs

2 tbsp chopped blueberry leaves
250ml (8fl oz/1 cup) water, just boiled
honey, to taste

Place the leaves in a cup of water. Leave to infuse for 5 minutes, then strain. Sweeten with honey to taste. Drink 1 cup every 4 hours.

banana

PROPERTIES/ACTIONS
- Nourishing
- Energizing
- Soothing

PARTS USED
- Whole fruit

BANANA SKIN POULTICE
for corns & calluses

**2 small, unripe banana skins
strip of cloth**

Using the cloth, bandage a piece of unripe banana skin, gummy-side down, onto the corn. Leave overnight and discard in the morning. Repeat the following night. After 2 days soak the feet in hot water, then scrape away the softened corn with a pumice stone. Repeat as necessary.

Bananas are packed with nourishing nutrients, particularly the mineral potassium, and have a long history of use as a natural energizer.

Because bananas are rich in potassium, they are a great energy food. They lower blood pressure and protect against heart disease by maintaining fluid balance and preventing plaque from sticking to artery walls. Bananas are also rich in fibre, and are therefore highly beneficial to the digestive tract, soothing and helping to restore normal function after constipation or diarrhoea. They act as antacids, useful for heartburn or ulcers. Banana skins can soften corns and calluses.

The horticulture employed on banana plantations has its origins in prehistoric times.

papaya

First used in Mayan medicine, papayas have beautiful yellow-orange flesh and are packed with carotenoids, helpful for many diseases.

Papaya comes out on top in the antioxidant stakes, with half a fruit providing a whopping 38 milligrams of powerful carotenoids. It can thus help to protect against cancer and cardiovascular disease, and to treat skin irritations.

Papaya contains protease enzymes similar to those present in the stomach, therefore favouring healthy digestion. The fruit is a mild diuretic, and is particularly useful in treating children's urinary and digestive ailments.

PROPERTIES/ACTIONS
- Protective
- Promotes healthy digestion
- Diuretic

PARTS USED
- Whole fruit

PAPAYA-MINT SALSA

1 under-ripe papaya, peeled and seeded
3 small carrots, peeled
4 spring onions
1 lemon and 2 limes
4 drops green Tabasco sauce
2 tsp vegetable oil
1 tsp salt
pinch of black pepper
15g (½oz/½ cup) coarsely chopped fresh mint leaves

Finely chop the papaya, carrots and spring onions and place in a bowl. Toss together. Using a sharp knife, remove the peel and pith from the lemon. Section and chop the lemon and 1 lime. Add to the mixture, then squeeze the juice from the remaining lime into the bowl. Add the Tabasco sauce, oil, salt, pepper and mint. Toss together to combine.

spinach

As every admirer of Popeye knows, spinach is nature's own source of iron. It has many other health-giving qualities.

Spinach is best eaten raw as cooking strips it of its carotenoid nutrients.

PROPERTIES/ACTIONS
- Rich in iron
- Rich in chlorophyll

PARTS USED
- Leaves

The high iron content of spinach makes it good for anaemia. It is also rich in the dark green plant "blood" chlorophyll, which benefits those suffering from general fatigue and is also thought to help fight cancer.

Spinach is an anti-inflammatory and a diuretic, and can be used for constipation and night blindness. It is also rich in B-complex vitamins and is calming for the nervous system. It has emollient properties, helping to soften surface tissues.

SPINACH POULTICE
for calluses & heel spurs

40g (1½ oz/1 cup) raw spinach leaves, crushed
gauze bandage

Wrap the spinach leaves in the bandage and tie to the affected area. Leave for 20 minutes, then discard. Repeat as necessary to soften and soothe inflamed or hardened tissue.

cauliflower

Like other members of the cabbage (Cruciferae) family, cauliflower is loaded with nutrients that seem to wage war against a host of diseases.

Cauliflower is a rich source of phytonutrients, thought to help stave off cancer. Sulforaphane steps up the production of enzymes that sweep toxins out of the body, while Indole-3-carbinol reduces levels of harmful oestrogens that can foster tumour growth, particularly in the breast and prostate gland.

Cauliflower is also packed with vitamin C and folate, which are known for keeping the immune system strong.

Cauliflower should be avoided by those with gout as it contains uric acid-forming purines.

PROPERTIES/ACTIONS
- Anti-cancer
- Boosts immunity

PARTS USED
- Vegetable head

MEDITERRANEAN-STYLE CAULIFLOWER

1 medium cauliflower
60ml (2fl oz/¼ cup) water
5 black olives, pitted and minced
1 tbsp minced fresh parsley
1 tsp red wine vinegar
pinch crushed red pepper flakes

Put the cauliflower and water in a saucepan. Cover and bring to the boil. Cook for 4 to 5 minutes, or until the cauliflower starts to soften. Stir in the olives, parsley, vinegar and pepper flakes. Cook for 1 minute or until heated through.

avocado

With many different varieties, the avocado is a healthful fruit with a long and detailed history dating from the ancient world to modern times.

PROPERTIES/ACTIONS
- High in monounsaturated fats
- Controls cholesterol
- Rich in folate
- Soothes the nervous system

PARTS USED
- Avocado flesh

A type of pear, avocados are high in monounsaturated fats and fibre, and they help to control cholesterol, improve the circulatory system and enrich the skin. They are rich in folate, which helps to prevent birth defects, and potassium, which staves off fatigue, depression, heart disease and strokes.

> The earliest use of avocado has been recorded at an 8th-century site in Peru.

Avocados are antioxidant dense and are said to have a unique anti-bacterial and anti-fungal substance in the pulp. They harmonize the liver and soothe the nervous system.

GUACAMOLE

3 medium, ripe avocados
1 tomato, diced
½ small onion, minced
1 garlic clove, minced and mashed with ½ tsp salt
1 small red chilli, deseeded and finely chopped (optional)
1 ½ tbsp fresh lemon juice

2 tbsp chopped fresh coriander
black pepper

Halve the avocados and scoop out the flesh into a bowl. Add the remaining ingredients and mix well until almost smooth. Season with black pepper to taste.

beetroot

A powerful blood cleanser and tonic, the root vegetable beetroot is an ancient remedy for a number of conditions.

With its cleansing properties, beetroot promotes a healthy digestive system. It is also high in assimilable iron, and may therefore help conditions such as anaemia, heart problems, constipation and liver toxicity, as well as restlessness and anxiety. Because of its striking ability to increase cellular uptake of oxygen and its anti-carcinogenic substances, beetroot is also thought to help fight cancer.

PROPERTIES/ACTIONS
• Cleansing
• Treats anaemia
• Nervine
• Blood builder

PARTS USED
• Whole vegetable

CHILLED BEETROOT SOUP

900g (30oz/5½ cups) beetroots, cooked
2 tbsp red wine vinegar
1 tsp light brown sugar
4 tbsp sour cream
75g (2½oz/½ cup) cucumbers, diced
1 tbsp chopped fresh dill

Peel and dice the beetroot and blend in a food processor. Add the vinegar and sugar. Process for 1–2 minutes into a chunky purée. Transfer to a bowl and chill in the refrigerator for up to 12 hours. Top each serving with 1 tablespoon sour cream, cucumber and dill.

PROPERTIES/ACTIONS
- Anti-cancer
- High in fibre

PARTS USED
- Whole vegetable

potato

Simple yet versatile, the potato is the world's number one vegetable crop and has long been used as a folk remedy.

Potatoes are a good source of complex carbohydrates, which help maintain blood sugar levels and boost energy. They are also high in vitamin C, which boosts immunity, and due to their potassium content they can help to control high blood pressure. Being rich in fibre they offer additional digestive benefits. The outer peel of potatoes contains chlorogenic acid, which acts as an anti-carcinogenic compound.

Its kinship with the deadly nightshade family made the potato feared when first discovered.

POTATO JUICE
for healthy digestion

250g (9oz) potatoes
lemon juice, to taste

Peel and scrub the potatoes, then chop into bite-sized pieces before liquidizing. Add lemon juice to taste. Take 2 tablespoons before each meal. Do not take the juice for longer than 24 hours.

squash

Judging by the remains found in Mexican caves, we have been eating squash, which is packed full of beta-carotene, for at least 7,000 years.

Winter squashes such as butternut squash are full of beta-carotene and vitamin C, antioxidant vitamins that have been shown to help prevent cancer and certain age-related conditions. High levels of potassium and magnesium, combined with insoluble fibre, also make squash a great food for lowering cholesterol and preventing high blood pressure, strokes and heart attacks.

PROPERTIES/ACTIONS
• Rich in beta-carotene
• Packed with vitamin C
• Lowers cholesterol

PARTS USED
• Squash flesh

BUTTERNUT SQUASH SOUFFLÉ

800g (1lb 12oz/4 cups) squash, peeled and diced
250ml (8fl oz/1 cup) water
½ tsp salt
70g (2½oz) butter, melted
175g (6oz/1 cup) brown sugar
½ tsp cinnamon
½ cup evaporated milk
50g (1¾oz) marshmallows

Preheat the oven to 180°C/350°F/Gas Mark 4. Simmer the squash, water and salt for 15 minutes. Drain, then mash. Add the remaining ingredients. Bake in a greased soufflé dish for 30 minutes.

celery

With its roots in 16th-century Italy, celery, a member of the parsley family, can stimulate the kidneys and help flush out the system.

PROPERTIES/ACTIONS
- Stimulates kidneys
- Nervine
- Sedative

PARTS USED
- Whole vegetable

Celery is good at aiding the elimination of waste via the urine, thus acting as a detoxifying agent. It is an anti-inflammatory, clearing uric acid from painful joints, and is well known as a remedy for gout and rheumatism. Celery is a useful antiseptic in the urinary tract and may help to lower blood pressure and prevent cancer. Celery seeds are more potent than other parts of the plant.

CELERY SEED TEA
for rheumatism & urinary infections

1 heaped tsp celery seeds
2 cups water

Place the seeds and water in an aluminium or a stainless steel pan. Bring to the boil, then remove from the heat and leave to infuse for 10 minutes. Strain. Drink up to 3 times a day depending on the severity of symptoms.

asparagus

In mythology asparagus has been renowned since ancient times both as an aphrodisiac and medicinally, for its healing properties.

With its active compound asparagine stimulating the kidneys, bladder and liver, asparagus is a powerful diuretic. Its anti-inflammatory action helps treat rheumatoid arthritis and its high fibre content inhibits bacterial growth in the intestines, thus staving off conditions such as irritable bowel syndrome.

Asparagus is an excellent source of folic acid, which is said to prevent birth defects. It also contains various antioxidants to fight cancerous cells and cardiovascular disease.

PROPERTIES/ACTIONS
- Diuretic
- Stimulating

PARTS USED
- Asparagus spears

Ancient Egyptian tomb drawings suggest that asparagus was grown in 4000 BC.

ASPARAGUS TINCTURE
for inflammatory conditions

10 young asparagus spears
500ml (17fl oz/2 cups) vodka

Chop the asparagus and place in a glass jar. Immerse in vodka and seal the jar tightly. Stand in a dark, cool place for 10 days, then discard the asparagus. Take 8–10 drops with a tablespoon of water three times a day, as needed.

artichoke

PROPERTIES/ACTIONS
- Protects liver
- Supports gallbladder

PARTS USED
- Leaves & heart

ARTICHOKE TINCTURE

150g (5½oz/5½ cups) dried
  artichoke leaves
300ml (10fl oz/½pt) alcohol,
  preferably vodka
600ml (20fl oz/1pt) water

Remove the leaves. Dry them
individually, then grind them
as finely as possible. Place
the ground leaves in a glass jar.
Cover with the alcohol and then
the water. Seal the jar tightly
and leave in a dark, cool place
for 2 weeks, shaking daily.
Strain the liquid through a fine
cheesecloth into a dark glass
bottle. Take 5–30 drops three
times a day, as needed.

Recognized mostly for its detoxifying effects,
globe artichoke protects the liver and supports
the gallbladder, making it a useful vegetable in
many traditional remedies.

Originating in the Mediterranean, artichokes are the unopened
flower buds of a thistle-like perennial plant. Each bud consists
of several parts: overlapping outer leaves that are tough and
inedible at the tip, but fleshy and tender at the base; an inedible
choke, or thistle, which is enclosed within a light-coloured
cone of immature leaves; and a round, firm-fleshed base,
known as the heart. Collectively, artichokes contain vitamin C,
high levels of B vitamins, dietary fibre, and a multitude of
minerals. Both the leaves and heart have a long history of
therapeutic use.

Containing an active ingredient called cynarin, artichokes,
particularly the leaves, can help the liver to cope with an
onslaught of rich party food and excess alcohol by maintaining
a steady flow of bile – a fluid that helps the body to digest fats.
Since artichokes are also a rich source of energy, taking the
tincture is a great way to help to cure a hangover.

Because of their detoxifying qualities, artichokes are also a
useful addition to the diet of people suffering from conditions

like gout, arthritis and rheumatism. Traditionally, artichokes have been used to help to control blood cholesterol and to lower blood sugar. The hearts are particularly good for helping to combat indigestion if eaten at the beginning of a meal.

Make sure you wash artichokes thoroughly as dirt often gets between the leaves.

sweet potato

Discovered by Columbus in the West Indies, orange-fleshed sweet potatoes are packed full of beta-carotene and other nutrients.

Sweet potatoes are rich in both beta-carotene and vitamin C, which boost immunity and help to prevent cardiovascular disease. These two powerful antioxidants also stave off some age-related conditions, particularly those of the eyes.

Beta-carotene can reduce the risk of cancer, especially endometrial cancer, while for those with respiratory problems, vitamin C acts on the lining of the lungs and makes breathing easier. Sweet potatoes are a complex carbohydrate and are rich in fibre, and can thus help to maintain blood-sugar levels.

PROPERTIES/ACTIONS
- Boosts immunity
- Anti-cancer
- Complex carbohydrate
- Rich in fibre

PARTS USED
- Whole vegetable

SWEET POTATO CAKES

200g (7oz/2 cups) sweet potato, cooked, with skin removed
100g (3½oz/1 cup) buckwheat flour
100g (3½oz/1 cup) margarine
1 apple, grated
1 tsp chopped ginger

Preheat the oven to 200°C/375°F/Gas Mark 5. Combine the ingredients. Form into 4–8 balls, arrange on a greased baking sheet and flatten slightly. Bake for 30 minutes. Eat warm.

carrot

Arriving in Britain as early as the 16th century, carrots have become well known for their cleansing effect on the blood and liver, and for their ability to aid vision.

Carrots contain high levels of beta-carotene which, besides giving them their reputation for aiding vision, also promotes healthy digestion and protects against cancer. Carrots are also full of antioxidant vitamins A, C and E, helping to fight heart disease. They are recommended for liver problems, increasing red blood cells and treating jaundice, as well as eczema. Their chromium content can help to stabilize blood-sugar levels.

PROPERTIES/ACTIONS
- Aids vision
- Treats liver & blood
- Anti-cancer

PARTS USED
- Whole vegetable

In the 1st century AD Dioscorides said that carrot seeds "wake up the genital virtue".

VITALITY-BOOSTING CARROT JUICE

3 carrots, unpeeled
2 apples, unpeeled
1 small beetroot, unpeeled

Prepare each ingredient by cleaning and chopping into chunks. Press through a juicer and drink immediately.

cabbage

Packed with antioxidants and cancer-fighting compounds, cabbages were used in ancient therapeutic rituals in Greek and Roman times.

Cabbages are rich in antioxidant nutrients like vitamin C and beta-carotene, which can boost immunity, reduce blood pressure and fight heart disease. Cabbages also provide folate, and may therefore help to reduce birth defects.

Cabbages contain indole-3-carbinol, or 13C, which sweeps up harmful oestrogens linked to breast cancer. Another compound found in cabbages, sulforaphane, has been shown to block prostate and colon cancer by stepping up the production of tumour-preventing enzymes.

PROPERTIES/ACTIONS
- Anti-cancer
- High in antioxidants
- Relieves inflammation

PARTS USED
- Leaves

RAW CABBAGE POULTICE
for inflammation (arthritis, mastitis)

5 inside raw cabbage leaves
3 tbsp chamomile tea
soft cotton cloth

Mince the cabbage leaves into small pieces and place in a bowl. Add 3 tablespoons of hot chamomile tea and combine. Roll in the cloth and apply to the inflamed area. Leave for 5 minutes. Repeat as required.

broccoli

A member of the cabbage family (Cruciferae), broccoli has ancient beginnings. It has been shown to aid many conditions, including cancer.

Broccoli contains a number of chemical compounds, including indoles, carotenoids and the vitamin A precursor beta-carotene, known to inhibit the activation of cancer cells.

High in antioxidants, including vitamin C, broccoli is known to help boost immunity and prevent conditions such as heart disease and osteoporosis. It is rich in iron and therefore helps to treat anaemia, and is a good source of fibre.

PROPERTIES/ACTIONS
- Anti-cancer
- Boosts immunity

PARTS USED
- Vegetable head

WARM BROCCOLI & SESAME SALAD

1 head broccoli florets
2 tbsp olive oil
60ml (2fl oz/¼ cup) soy sauce
60ml (2fl oz/¼ cup) rice wine
    vinegar
2 tbsp sesame oil
4 tbsp sesame seeds, toasted

Preheat the oven to 200°C/375°F/Gas Mark 5. Blanch the broccoli for 1 minute. Drain, spread on a baking tray and coat with olive oil. Roast for 10 minutes. Transfer to a bowl. Whisk the soy sauce, vinegar and sesame oil. Stir in 3 tablespoons sesame seeds. Pour over the broccoli. Sprinkle with remaining seeds.

mushroom
(shiitake & maitake)

Mushrooms are a fungus supplying key nutrients to stimulate the immune system and prevent high cholesterol, and perhaps even cancer and AIDS.

PROPERTIES/ACTIONS
- Boosts immunity
- Anti-cancer
- Calming

PARTS USED
- Whole vegetable

Shiitake mushrooms in particular contain nutrients that have proved to be effective in bolstering the immune system. Maitake mushrooms contain beta-glucan, which stops HIV from killing white blood cells, possibly preventing AIDS. Beta-glucan is also highly effective in shrinking cancerous tumours. Shiitake mushrooms contain eritadenine, thought to lower cholesterol, and all mushrooms are high in B vitamins.

STUFFED MUSHROOMS

4 large mushrooms
4 tbsp olive oil
4 spring onions, chopped
1 red pepper, deseeded and finely chopped
2 small courgettes, chopped
8 green olives, pitted and chopped
2 tbsp porridge oats
1 tbsp chopped basil
1 tbsp soy sauce

Preheat the oven to 180°C/ 350°F/Gas Mark 4. De-stalk the mushrooms. Heat the oil in a saucepan and gently fry the onions, pepper, courgettes, olives and oats for 3 minutes. Stir in the basil and soy sauce. Place the mushrooms on a baking tray and spoon the mixture over them. Bake for 15–20 minutes. Serve on a bed of salad.

tomato

A favourite ingredient in many dishes, this juicy, sumptuous fruit was discovered by the early Aztecs of South America and is recognized today for its cancer-preventing nutrients.

Tomatoes are filled with the antioxidant vitamins C and E, as well as beta-carotene. They can help to prevent everything from cataracts to heart disease and cancer.

Lycopene, which gives tomatoes their vivid red colour, may also lower the risk of cancer, particularly cancer of the prostate, breast, lung and endometrium. This nutrient additionally helps people to stay active for longer.

PROPERTIES/ACTIONS
- Boots immunity
- Fights cancer

PARTS USED
- Whole tomato

Red, ripe tomatoes can have four times more beta-carotene than green, immature ones.

SUN-DRIED TOMATO PESTO

24 sun-dried tomatoes, pre-soaked in oil
75g (3oz/⅝ cup) macadamia nuts, chopped
150g (5oz/5 cups) fresh basil leaves
3 garlic cloves, crushed
½ tbsp tomato purée
22ml (¾oz/½ tbsp) balsamic vinegar
3 tsp lemon juice
250ml (8fl oz/1 cup) tomato juice
4 tbsp olive oil
salt and pepper, to taste

Blend all the ingredients together in a food processor until smooth. Transfer to a bowl and season to taste. Store for up to 5 days in the refrigerator.

watercress

With its pungent, peppery flavour, leafy green watercress packs a significant punch as a traditional spring tonic.

A member of the crucifer family, watercress is well known for its cancer-fighting potential. Its phenethyl isothiocyanate compound is particularly potent against lung cancer and bronchitis caused by tobacco smoke. Watercress is a good source of iodine – useful for those with low thyroid activity. It is a diuretic and has expectorant and depurative properties, therefore easing inflammation, ulcers and boils.

PROPERTIES/ACTIONS
- Anti-cancer
- Expectorant
- Diuretic

PARTS USED
- Leaves & stalks

CREAMY WATERCRESS SOUP

2 bunches watercress, chopped
1 medium onion, peeled and
   diced
50g (2oz/¼ cup) butter
25g (1oz/¼ cup) plain flour
500ml (1 pint/2 cups) milk
450ml (1 pint/2 cups) vegetable
   stock
6 tbsp single cream

Melt the butter and gently fry the watercress and onion for 3 minutes. Stir in the flour and cook for 1 minute. Slowly add the milk and then the stock, while stirring. Bring to the boil and stir until thickened. Cover and simmer for 30 minutes. Whizz the mixture in a blender, then add the cream and reheat gently without boiling. Serve.

onion

A member of the allium family, onions have long played a central role in folk medicine and have a wealth of health-giving properties.

Onions are known to protect the circulatory system – they contain many compounds that help lower cholesterol, thin the blood and prevent the hardening of arteries. Rich in quercetin, onions may halt the progression of cancerous tumours and eliminate harmful bacteria in the gut. They also contain sulphur compounds that inhibit the inflammatory response, thus treating everything from insect bites to asthma.

PROPERTIES/ACTIONS
- Protective
- Expectorant
- Anti-cancer
- Antibiotic

PARTS USED
- Whole vegetable, peeled

In medieval Europe bunches of onions were hung on doors to help ward off the plague.

ONION COMPRESS *for inflamed wounds, headaches & earaches*

4 medium onions, peeled and finely chopped
white muslin or linen bag

Lightly steam the onions and wrap in the white muslin or linen bag. Apply to the inflamed area or aching parts. Once the compress cools down, replace it with another. Repeat up to four times in succession, or until the symptoms alleviate.

chilli

According to traditional Oriental theory, "If you have a cold, you can build a fire in your stomach" with a spice such as chilli.

Chilli is a hot, pungent yang spice and a highly effective decongestant for colds as well as respiratory disorders. It flushes out the sinuses and clears the lungs, thus treating various bronchial conditions.

Chilli also acts on the circulatory and digestive systems, and is used to treat a wide range of complaints ranging from arthritis and chilblains to colic and diarrhoea.

PROPERTIES/ACTIONS
- Stimulant
- Carminative
- Antiseptic
- Expectorant
- Decongestant
- Analgesic

PARTS USED
- Fresh & dried chilli

CHILLI PASTE
for colds & bronchial conditions

3 small Thai dried chillis
2 garlic cloves, halved
1 small onion, chopped
30g (1oz) sugar
50ml (1½fl oz) lemon juice
50ml (1½fl oz) water
½ tsp salt

Put the ingredients in a blender and whizz until finely chopped. Pour the mixture into a small pan and cook gently, stirring occasionally, for 10 minutes. Makes 100ml paste.

If you want the medicinal benefits but cannot stand the heat, try a little chilli at a time.

lentil

A staple food in many countries, lentils have a rich history of use and are one of the single best-known, nutritious and digestible foods.

Whether red, green or brown, lentils are a good source of protein. They contain high levels of B vitamins, particularly B3, deficiency of which can lead to poor memory and irritability. They are also rich in iron and are recommended for pregnant and lactating women, as well as those suffering from anaemia.

Lentils are a good source of fibre and help to regulate colon function, as well as the circulatory system.

PROPERTIES/ACTIONS
- High in protein
- Regulates nervous system
- Rich in fibre

PARTS USED
- Whole lentil

SPICY LENTIL BURGERS

175g (6oz/⅞ cup) red lentils
1 tbsp olive oil
1 onion, finely chopped
1–2 tsp curry powder
**450ml (16fl oz/2 cups)
    vegetable stock**
**125g (4oz/1 cup) wholemeal
    breadcrumbs**

Fry the onion in the oil, then stir in the curry powder and cook for 2 minutes. Add the lentils and stock. Bring to the boil, then simmer for 20–25 minutes. Add the breadcrumbs and shape into four burgers. Grill on a lightly oiled baking tray until crisp and brown.

soya bean

033

PROPERTIES/ACTIONS
- Rich in protein
- Lowers cholesterol
- Source of phyto-oestrogens
- Low GI
- Combats stress

PARTS USED
- Whole bean

Originating in Japan, soya beans are made into a number of food products with a wealth of ancient medicinal properties.

Soya beans can be included in the diet in the form of soya oil, soya flour, tofu, tempeh, soya milk, textured vegetable protein (TVP), miso and soya sauce, and are often used instead of meat or dairy protein. Being rich in lecithin, a natural emulsifier of fats, they can assist in lowering cholesterol levels. Plant-derived protein is also said to help guard against gallstones.

Perhaps best known for their phyto-oestrogen content, soya beans are said to reduce symptoms of menopause and osteoporosis. They are excellent in promoting healthy colon

---

SOYA BEAN PÂTÉ

200g (7oz/1 cup) soya beans, pre-cooked
1 tbsp olive oil
1 medium onion, finely chopped
2 tbsp tomato purée
10 black olives, pitted and chopped

2 tbsp chopped fresh parsley
1 tbsp sesame seeds, lightly toasted
pinch of salt

Put the soya beans in a bowl and mash them with a fork. Heat the olive oil in a frying pan and sauté the onion until it is clear and soft. Add to the beans. Stir in the tomato purée, olives, parsley, sesame seeds and salt. Chill for at least 30 minutes before serving.

and bowel function, and are protective against constipation, diverticular disease and haemorrhoids.

Soya beans have a low glycaemic index (GI) and are great blood sugar and insulin regulators, which makes them useful in maintaining energy levels and for diabetics. They are also a valuable source of B-complex vitamins, which support the nervous system and help to combat stress.

SOYA PANCAKES

125g (4½oz/1 cup) soya flour
345g (12oz/2¾ cups) plain flour
3 tbsp baking powder
3 tbsp sugar
½ tsp salt
3 eggs
750ml (24fl oz/3 cups) soya milk
6 tbsp soya oil
knob of butter

Combine all the ingredients, except the butter, in a bowl and beat to form a batter. Melt the butter in a frying pan and add ½ cup of batter. Cook on both sides until golden brown. Fold and serve.

aduki bean

Nutty in flavour, aduki beans are popular in Japan, where they have been used for their healing properties for more than 1,000 years.

According to Oriental medicine, aduki beans help to disperse stagnant blood, which can be the cause of many diseases. They have a tonifying effect on the kidney-adrenal function and therefore help to regulate the stress response.

Aduki beans are diuretic and drying in nature, and are useful in the treatment of conditions like diarrhoea, oedema and boils. They are also good for the urinary tract.

PROPERTIES/ACTIONS
- Disperses stagnant blood
- Tonifying
- Diuretic

PARTS USED
- Whole bean

ADUKI BEAN SOUP

200g (7oz/1 cup) dried aduki beans
600ml (1 pint/2½ cups) vegetable stock
1 medium onion, sliced
1 carrot, diced
1 celery stick, diced
soy sauce, to taste

Put all the ingredients, except the soy sauce, in a saucepan. Bring to the boil, then simmer for 1 hour, or until the vegetables are tender. Add the soy sauce to taste. Blend in a food processor if desired.

black bean

Originating in Peru, black beans are often used in the Creole and Cajun cuisines of North America and are highly nutritious.

Black beans are a source of complex carbohydrates, useful for many ailments, including heart problems. Rich in iron, they are known to help anaemia and to impart strength when recovering from illness. They are a rich source of energy-providing potassium, as well as folate, which may lower the risk of heart disease and fight birth defects. They act on the reproductive organs and blood, and are useful for gynaecological problems.

PROPERTIES/ACTIONS
• Rich in iron
• Promotes reproductive health

PARTS USED
• Whole bean

BLACK BEAN DIP

300g (10½oz/1½ cups) black
    beans, cooked
1 small carrot, diced
1 small piece of celery, diced
1 tbsp garlic, minced
1 tsp dried oregano
1 tsp ground cumin
½ tsp ground coriander
¼ tsp salt
125g (4½ oz/½ cup) sour
    cream

Whizz all the ingredients in a blender. Transfer to a serving bowl. Cover and chill in the refrigerator until needed.

chickpea

Chickpeas are grown from the equatorial tropics to the temperate northern latitudes of Russia, and are among the most nutritious of pulses.

Chickpeas are a good source of isoflavones, which mimic oestrogen in the body. They can therefore help to prevent hormone-related conditions, including PMS and breast cancer. Chickpeas have antiseptic properties and are a diuretic, making them useful for cystitis and oedema.

They also aid the absorption of nutrients and are good for general digestive health. In addition, chickpeas support the functions of nerves and muscles in the body.

PROPERTIES/ACTIONS
- Mimics oestrogen
- Antiseptic
- Diuretic

PARTS USED
- Whole pulse

HUMMUS

225g (8oz/1 cup) canned chickpeas
4 cloves garlic, peeled
4 tbsp tahini
4 tbsp olive oil
2 lemons, cut in half

Drain the chickpeas and place them in a food processor, together with the garlic, tahini and olive oil. Squeeze the juice from the lemons and add to the mixture. Blend until pale and creamy. Top with a little olive oil, and serve as a dip with vegetable crudités.

almond

Steeped in history, these sweet, versatile nuts have a higher dietary fibre and calcium content than any other nut and help us to stay healthy.

Due to their relatively high fibre content, almonds help promote healthy digestion, while the calcium in them contributes to strong bones. Almonds also contain the phytochemicals quercetin and kaempferol, which may protect against cancer. With over 65 percent monounsaturated fats that help lower blood fat levels, and a high vitamin E content, almonds can keep LDL cholesterol from oxidizing and sticking to artery walls, thus providing protection from heart disease.

PROPERTIES/ACTIONS
- Promotes healthy digestion
- Heart protective
- Anti-cancer

PARTS USED
- Whole nut

ALMOND & RAISIN MILK

225g (8oz/2 cups) whole almonds (not roasted or salted)
water, for soaking
handful of dried raisins
455ml (16fl oz/2 cups) water

Cover the almonds with water and soak for 24 hours; drain and rinse. Soak the raisins in water for 2 hours; drain. Put the almonds, raisins and 455ml water in a food processor. Blend, then strain through a fine sieve. Keep in the refrigerator for up to 4 days.

pumpkin seed

Pumpkin seeds are nature's nutritious snack food, supplying plenty of zinc, iron, protein, essential fatty acids and B-complex vitamins.

Due to their high zinc content, pumpkin seeds have a reputation as a male sexual tonic and can reduce an enlarged prostate gland. They also provide a valuable source of energy through the presence of digestible iron.

Containing omega-3 fatty acids, pumpkin seeds are good for the skin and help boost memory-retentive cells. They may help to fight cardiovascular and immuno-deficiency disorders, and are useful in the treatment of intestinal parasites.

PROPERTIES/ACTIONS
- Promotes prostate health
- Fights fatigue
- Aids memory

PARTS USED
- Whole seed

PUMPKIN SEED PORRIDGE

300g (10½ oz/1½ cups) pumpkin seeds, unpeeled
500–750ml (16–24fl oz/2–3 cups) milk
honey, to taste

Grind the pumpkin seeds in a food processor or mill. Add 2 cups of milk and blend to form a porridge consistency. Add additional milk, as desired. Transfer to a saucepan and bring to the boil. Add honey to taste, and serve.

sunflower seed

Power-packed with a whole host of nutrients, sunflower seeds are one of the finest energy "pick-me-ups" that nature provides.

Sunflower seeds are a valuable source of B vitamins, which means they are nourishing to the adrenal glands and thus may help to combat energy slumps and many symptoms associated with stress.

The seeds' essential fatty acid content may be beneficial in treating eczema, as well as depression and irritability. Sunflower seeds are a diuretic and expectorant, and have been used in the treatment of bronchial, throat and lung infections.

PROPERTIES/ACTIONS
- Energizing
- Anti-stress
- Diuretic
- Expectorant

PARTS USED
- Whole seed

SEED TRAIL MIX

80g (2¾oz/½ cup) sunflower seeds
40g (1½oz/¼ cup) pumpkin seeds
30g (1oz/¼ cup) blanched almonds, finely chopped
90g (3 ¼oz/1 cup) flaked and toasted coconut
160g (5¼oz/⅓ cup) chopped dried apricots

Bake the seeds and nuts on a baking tray at 180°C/350°F/Gas Mark 4 for 4–5 minutes, until golden. Mix with the coconut and apricots.

Native Americans ground sunflower seeds to a meal for thickening soups and drinks.

*flaxseed

PROPERTIES/ACTIONS
- Rich source of EFAs
- Involved in energy production
- Good for reproductive health
- Expectorant

PARTS USED
- Whole seed

FLAXSEED POULTICE
for inflammation, congestion & pain

2 tbsp ground flaxseed
455ml (16fl oz/2 cups) water
linen cloth

Bring the flaxseed and water to the boil in a pan, then reduce the heat and stir until a thick paste forms. Spread onto the linen cloth and fold this over the paste. Apply the poultice to the affected area. Fix by wrapping another piece of cloth around it. To retain the heat for longer, wrap with a blanket.

With abundant and balanced levels of essential fatty acids, flaxseed is acclaimed in history for its ability to prevent and combat many conditions.

Today, the amazing health-giving virtues of flaxseed are recognized throughout the world.

High in both omega-3 and omega-6 essential fatty acids (EFAs), flaxseeds are involved in systematic energy production, oxygen transfer and transportation of fats, and may therefore

help to maintain the body's tissue cells, reproductive organs, glands, muscles and eyes. Flaxseed is thus traditionally used to treat everything from malnutrition and skin diseases, to arthritis, PMS and fertility problems. Essential fatty acids are also needed to make prostaglandins, hormone-like substances responsible for stamina, circulation and metabolism. Flaxseed can therefore help to maintain healthy blood fat levels and prevent cardiovascular disease.

Flaxseed is expectorant and dissolving by nature and may help to treat conditions such as coughs and bronchitis, as well as other inflammatory ailments. The seeds also have a mild purgative action and can be capable of tonifying the bowel, easing constipation.

The ancient Abyssinians were probably the first humans to use flaxseeds for food.

Brazil nut

Large seeds of giant trees that grow in South America's Amazon jungle, Brazil nuts provide a plethora of healing nutrients.

PROPERTIES/ACTIONS
- Boosts mood
- Anti-cancer
- Lowers cholesterol

PARTS USED
- Whole nut

Well known for their selenium content, Brazil nuts may protect against breast cancer as well as depression. They are high in protein, as well as in vitamin B1 and magnesium, which are both essential to the nervous system.

High in unsaturated fat, Brazil nuts can help lower cholesterol, while their arginine and flavonoid content may provide protection against coronary disease and cancer.

BRAZIL NUT BRITTLE

440g (15½oz/2 cups) granulated sugar
¼ tsp bicarbonate of soda
190g (6¾oz/1½ cups) ground Brazil nuts
175g (6oz) milk chocolate, melted

In a heavy frying pan, melt the sugar over a low heat, stirring. Add the soda and 1 cup of the nuts, and mix. Roll out on a greased baking sheet until about ½cm (¼in) thick. When cold, cover with chocolate and sprinkle with remaining nuts. Once set, break into pieces.

brown rice

As well as being the dietary staple of the East, brown rice is a folk remedy for soothing the digestive and circulatory systems.

Brown rice contains abundant amounts of fibre, which promotes healthy digestion. It also has a soothing effect on the entire intestinal tract, helping to ease conditions like irritable bowel syndrome. Short-grain rice varieties are good for colon function, helping to clear toxic waste.

Also rich in B vitamins, brown rice helps to relieve anxiety, fatigue and depression. The outer layer of the grain, the bran, contains oryzanol, which lowers cholesterol. Externally, rice can help to alleviate skin conditions, including inflammation.

PROPERTIES/ACTIONS
- Soothes digestive tract
- Reduces cholesterol
- Relives fatigue

PARTS USED
- Whole grain

It is believed that the roots of rice were discovered in India around 3000 BC.

GROUND RICE POULTICE
for skin inflammation

40g (1½oz/⅛ cup) ground brown rice
60ml (2fl oz/¼ cup) milk
gauze or cotton strip

In a bowl, mix the rice and milk to make a paste. Apply to the affected area. Bandage securely in place, using the gauze or cotton strip. Leave on for up to 3 hours, as required.

quinoa

Pronounced "keenwa", and introduced from the South American Andes, quinoa is rich in unique health-sustaining properties.

Quinoa contains significantly more protein than any other grain and is especially well suited to children and to those suffering from anaemia or even muscular degeneration. It is also cleansing to the arterial system and is rich in nutrients, especially calcium, iron, B-complex vitamins and vitamin E. In Eastern medicine quinoa is used to strengthen the kidneys and revitalize the liver, and for everything from reproductive health and urinary problems to detoxification and skin disorders.

PROPERTIES/ACTIONS
- Complete food
- Cleansing
- Strengthening

PARTS USED
- Whole grain

> Quinoa, along with corn and potatoes, was considered the centrepiece of the Andean diet.

SOUTH-WESTERN QUINOA & CHICKPEA SALAD

90g (3¼oz/1 cup) quinoa
500ml (17fl oz/2 cups) water
4 tsp olive oil
225g (8oz/1 cup) canned
  chickpeas, drained
1 medium tomato, seeded and
  chopped
3 tbsp lime juice
2 tbsp minced fresh coriander
½ tsp ground cumin

1 garlic clove, minced
pinch of salt

Bring the quinoa and water to the boil in a saucepan, reduce the heat, cover and simmer for 15 minutes. Drain and transfer the quinoa to a bowl. Drizzle with oil and toss. Add the remaining ingredients and mix well.

rye

Grown in Russia for more than 2,000 years, rye is commonly milled into flour and is used as a nutritious alternative to wheat.

High in calcium, iron and potassium, the rye grain is good for osteoporosis, anaemia and headaches. It is also rich in plant lignans, which help to reduce blood viscosity. Containing dietary fibre, rye may relieve constipation. Rye also contains sucrose and fructooligosaccharide, which have prebiotic properties that are useful to digestive health.

PROPERTIES/ACTIONS
- Rich in calcium & iron
- Highly digestible
- Prebiotic qualities

PARTS USED
- Whole grain

RYE PANCAKES

100g (3½oz/⅔ cup) rye flour
1 large egg
100ml (3½fl oz/½ cup) water
150ml (¼ pint/⅔ cup) milk
1 tbsp olive oil

Whizz the rye flour, egg, water and milk in a food processor. Leave to stand for 10–15 minutes. Drizzle some oil into a heavy frying pan and heat. Carefully ladle in the batter, allowing 2–3 tablespoons per pancake. As the mixture for each pancake begins to bubble on the surface, flip it over and leave for 4–5 minutes, or until cooked through.

Rye evolved with wheat and barley for more than 2,000 years until its value became recognized.

buckwheat

A staple in Russia and Poland, buckwheat, although commonly considered a grain, is, in fact, a nut with unique health-giving abilities.

Buckwheat is high in the bioflavonoid rutin, which strengthens blood capillaries and is an especially good food for the prevention and treatment of varicose veins, frostbite and chilblains. Rutin may be particularly important in the treatment of high blood pressure and hardening of the arteries, and it is also thought to lift depression.

Applied topically, buckwheat helps to draw out excess fluid from the tissues, thus helping to relieve pain and inflammation.

BUCKWHEAT POULTICE
for skin inflammation

220g (7½oz/1⅓ cup) buckwheat flour
250ml (8fl oz/1 cup) water
piece of muslin

Boil the water in a saucepan. Allow to cool a little, then add the flour and mix well to form a paste. Wrap the paste in the muslin. Apply directly to the affected area and hold in place with a bandage. Leave for 10 minutes, or until the paste begins to cool, then reheat and apply for another 10 minutes.

046

barley

A staple in the Middle Ages, barley is valued as a traditional remedy for its demulcent qualities and ability to cleanse the lymphatic system.

Barley has a unique ability to act on the mucous membranes, and may therefore help to soothe inflammatory conditions of the intestines and the urinary tract. Barley is rich in minerals, with high levels of calcium and potassium and plenty of B-complex vitamins, and it is useful for people suffering from stress or fatigue. It also contains beta-glucan, a gummy fibre that has dramatic cholesterol-lowering abilities.

Dioscorides said that barley could "weaken and restrain all sore and ulcerated throats".

PROPERTIES/ACTIONS
- Demulcent
- Cleansing
- Anti-stress

PARTS USED
- Whole grain

LEMON BARLEY WATER
for cystitis, constipation & diarrhoea

**125g (4oz/⅔ cup) pearl barley
900ml (2 pints/4 cups) water
grated zest of 1 lemon
honey, to taste**

Bring the pearl barley to a boil in a saucepan with 240ml (½ pint/1 cup) of the water. Strain, then add the remaining water and the lemon zest. Simmer until the barley is soft, adding water as required. Strain the liquid, sweeten with honey and leave to cool. Drink the lemon barley water when symptoms arise.

oats

PROPERTIES/ACTIONS

- Nerve tonic
- Eases digestive problems
- Anti-depressant
- Prevents heart disease
- Anti-spasmodic
- Emollient

PARTS USED

- Whole grain

OATEN JELLY
for gastric problems

65g (2½oz/½ cup) oat flour
450ml (16fl oz/2 cups) water
15g (½ oz) butter
sugar or honey, to taste

Blend the oat flour with a little water. Boil the rest of the water in a pan and slowly pour onto the flour, stirring until thick. Return the mixture to the pan and add the butter. Bring to the boil and simmer for 7 minutes, stirring continuously, until thick. Add sugar or honey.

Oats are highly nutritious and are a traditional remedy for soothing nervous conditions and aiding digestive complaints.

Although their native country is unknown, oats are said to be indigenous to Sicily and Chile. The grain is commonly "rolled" to be used as a commercial foodstuff, and when the seed is kiln dried, stripped of its husk and delicate outer skin, and then coarsely ground, it constitutes the oatmeal of Scotland.

Oats provide a cornucopia of nourishment – they are a good source of protein, and are incredibly high in calcium, potassium and magnesium which, like the B vitamins, act as a nerve tonic, as well as promoting strong bones and teeth. They are also rich in fibre and singularly digestible, as well as having a demulcent quality that protects the duodenal surfaces, stomach and intestines. Oats are especially good for irritable bowel syndrome since they are anti-spasmodic.

Oats have plenty of silicon for maintaining healthy arterial walls, and beta-glucan, a soluble fibre that overcomes high blood pressure. Oat bran, meanwhile, has become well known for combating high levels of blood cholesterol.

Oats are a complex carbohydrate with a very low glycaemic index (GI). They therefore provide sustainable energy, alleviating insomnia and improving insulin sensitivity in people with diabetes. They also have a mild tranquillizing effect, and are a reliable remedy for depression.

When applied locally, oats have an emollient effect, and when combined with water in the bath, they can help to alleviate skin irritations.

In 1652 Nicholas Culpeper said, "A poultice made of meal of oats and some oil of bay, helpeth the itch."

millet

Millet is a highly nutritious grain that supplies fantastic support to the digestive system, especially the stomach, spleen and pancreas.

PROPERTIES/ACTIONS
- Carminative
- Counteracts acidity
- Contains silicon

PARTS USED
- Whole grain

High in protein and low in starch, millet supports the digestive system as it is the only alkaline grain. It has anti-fungal and anti-mucus properties, which help to prevent ailments such as candida and premenstrual discomfort. Millet is rich in silicon, the great cleansing, mending and eliminating mineral salt, essential for hair, skin, teeth, eye and nail health. Silicon also supports arterial health. It has high levels of potassium and magnesium, useful for treating arthritis and osteoporosis.

SEASONAL VEGETABLE & MILLET STEW

375g (13oz/1½ cups) millet
1kg (2lb 4oz) seasonal
    vegetables of your choice,
    chopped into bite-size pieces
vegetable oil, for frying
2 litres (3½ pints/8 cups) boiling
    water
2 tsp vegetable bouillon powder

Place the vegetables in a large pan with a little oil and sauté until soft. Roast the millet separately in a little oil for 3–4 minutes, until brown. Add to the vegetables and sauté a little longer, stirring. Add the water and bouillon powder. Simmer for about 30 minutes. Add extra seasoning if desired. Serve hot.

liquorice

Liquorice has a wealth of healing properties, and the Chinese have been using this herb in traditional medicine for thousands of years.

Liquorice is a good remedy for lowering stomach-acid levels, so it may help to relieve over-acidity in the digestive tract and stomach ulcers. With its expectorant properties, it is useful for coughs, asthma and chest infections. The root contains glycyrrhizic acid, which gives the herb its anti-inflammatory, anti-allergenic and anti-arthritic actions. With an aspirin-like effect, it is helpful in relieving fevers and headaches. It also acts on the liver, increasing bile flow and lowering cholesterol.

Alexander the Great, Caesar and Brahma endorsed the properties of liquorice.

PROPERTIES/ACTIONS
- Lowers stomach acid
- Expectorant
- Anti-arthritic
- Aspirin-like effect

PARTS USED
- Root

LIQUORICE INFUSION
for coughs & chest complaints

25g (1oz) liquorice root
1 heaped tsp flaxseeds
110g (4oz/⅔ cup) raisins
2 litres (3½ pints/8 cups) water
110g (4oz/⅔ cup) brown sugar
1 tbsp white wine vinegar

Place the liquorice, flaxseed, raisins and water in a saucepan, and bring to the boil. Leave to simmer until the water has reduced by about half. Add the sugar and white wine vinegar, then stir well. Drink 240ml (½ pint/1 cup) before going to bed.

fennel

Part of the parsley family, the fennel plant and seeds have ancient medicinal properties and are also popular culinary ingredients.

Fennel is well known for its anti-spasmodic, analgesic and diuretic properties. It can be used to ease digestive problems, combat fluid retention and reduce intestinal spasms. Because it aids elimination of toxins through the urine, it is also a useful remedy for arthritis and gout. Its volatile oils have antiseptic effects, particularly useful for urinary infections.

PROPERTIES/ACTIONS
- Anti-spasmodic
- Diuretic
- Combats fluid retention
- Aids digestion

PARTS USED
- Seed

FENNEL & CLOVE MOUTHWASH

½ tsp fennel seeds
½ tsp ground cloves
2 tbsp pure grain alcohol or
   good-quality vodka
250ml (9fl oz/1 cup) distilled
   water
paper coffee filter

In a bowl, mix the spices into the alcohol. Cover and leave for 3 days, then pour through the coffee filter placed in a strainer. Add the water. Store in a sealed bottle for 6 weeks. Gargle with 1 tablespoon at a time, as a mouthwash.

In the Middle Ages fennel was considered to be an antidote to witchcraft.

echinacea

Also known as purple coneflower, there are various species of echinacea, all of which have been therapeutically effective throughout history.

Known as a non-specific immuno-stimulant, this herb has been shown to increase white blood cell count and promote respiratory cellular activity. It is used for colds, influenza, ear infections, chronic fatigue and allergies. Its anti-viral properties appear to be due to the stimulation of interferon-like effects. Traditionally, echinacea has also been used to promote healing and reduce inflammation, both internally for conditions such as colitis, and externally for ailments such as acne.

PROPERTIES/ACTIONS
- Immuno-stimulant
- Helps colds & influenza
- Promotes healing

PARTS USED
- Root

ECHINACEA THROAT DECOCTION

20g (¾oz) dried or 40g (1½oz) fresh echinacea root
750ml (24fl oz/3 cups) water

Place the echinacea root in a saucepan, cover with water and bring to the boil. Simmer for about 20–30 minutes, until the liquid has reduced by about one-third. Strain through a sieve into a jug. Discard the echinacea. Gargle about 50ml of liquid, either hot or cold, 3 times a day. Store in a cool place for up to 3 days.

peppermint

A well-known digestive aid, peppermint has many other benefits and is one of the most popular traditional remedies used today.

Peppermint soothes the digestive tract, and is used for heartburn, indigestion and nausea. It improves the circulation, and can help chills, fevers, colds, influenza, stuffiness and congestion. The herb also has analgesic properties, which are useful for headaches, inflamed joints, neuralgia and sciatica. The volatile oils have antiseptic properties, and are antibacterial, anti-parasitic, anti-fungal and anti-viral.

PEPPERMINT FOOT BATH
for tired feet

50g (2oz) fresh peppermint leaves, roughly chopped
1 litre (35fl oz/4 cups) boiling water
1.75 litres (44fl oz/7½ cups) hot water
1 tsp borax
1 tbsp Epsom salts

Combine the herbs with the boiling water in a large bowl. Leave for 1 hour, then strain. Add to a bowl or footbath filled with the hot water. Stir in the borax and Epsom salts. Soak the feet for 15–20 minutes.

053

rosemary

A potent, stimulating herb, rosemary is an old-fashioned remedy for everything from colds and colic, to nervousness and eczema.

Rosemary has antiseptic, antioxidant, anti-spasmodic and astringent qualities, proving useful for circulatory conditions, stiff muscles, coughs and colds, mouth and gum infections, and irritable bowel syndrome.

An invigorating herb, rosemary fights fatigue. It is also a nervine and is excellent for female complaints and headaches. The essential oil can be used as an insect repellent.

PROPERTIES/ACTIONS
- Astringent
- Anti-spasmodic
- Invigorating
- Nervine

PARTS USED
- Leaves

TONIC WINE & LINIMENT
for stiff muscles, headaches, etc

handful of fresh rosemary leaves
2 small cinnamon sticks
5 cloves
1 tsp ground ginger
bottle of good-quality red wine

Lightly crush the rosemary, cinnamon and cloves in a tall jar, using a pestle. Add the ginger, then the wine, seal the jar and leave in a cool place for 7–10 days. Strain and store in a sealed bottle. Drink a glass daily, or dip a cotton-wool pad and apply to the affected area.

Used in shampoos, rosemary is also reputed to prevent premature baldness.

sage

A native of the Mediterranean, this common garden plant is popular as a herb both used in cooking, and for its many curative properties.

With its fragrant aroma, sage has antiseptic, antibacterial and anti-viral properties, and is a traditional ingredient of cough, cold and respiratory remedies. With decongestant and astringent effects and an ability to reduce mucus, it is particularly successful in the treatment of bronchitis.

Sage stimulates the intestines and is a tonic for the digestive system. It also clears sluggish skin and firms tissues, is calming and soothing, and fights emotional distress.

PROPERTIES/ACTIONS
- Treats respiratory conditions
- Decongestant
- Digestive aid
- Calming & soothing

PARTS USED
- Leaves

SAGE & THYME GARGLE
for respiratory ailments

1 large handful sage leaves
1 small handful thyme leaves
450ml (16fl oz/2 cups) boiling water
30ml (1fl oz/2 tbsp) cider vinegar
2 tsp honey
1 tsp cayenne pepper

Roughly chop the leaves and place in a jug. Add the boiling water, cover and leave for 30 minutes. Strain off the leaves and stir in the cider vinegar, honey and cayenne. Gargle with the mixture at the first sign of symptoms, or drink 2 teaspoons 2 or 3 times a day. Use within a week.

dandelion

With healing properties in the roots, leaves and flowers, dandelion is a faithful folk remedy and one of the most frequently prescribed herbs.

Dandelion leaves are a powerful diuretic and are useful for bladder infections and oedema. The roots are a blood purifier, helping to remove toxins from the liver and kidneys. The leaves and roots produce mannitol, which is used for hypertension and a weak heart. An appetite stimulant, dandelion increases production of bile to help relieve digestive ailments. Rich in vitamins and iron, it is also useful for treating anaemia.

PROPERTIES/ACTIONS
- Diuretic
- Blood purifier
- Treats liver
- Increases bile production
- Rich in iron

PARTS USED
- Whole herb

DANDELION TONIC WINE

60g (2¼oz/1 cup) dandelion flowers
1 litre (34fl oz/4 cups) white wine
honey, to taste

Crush the flowers using a pestle and mortar, then place them in an airtight container. Pour in the white wine, seal the container and steep for 1 month, then strain out the flowers. Sweeten with honey, if desired. Drink 1 cup.

eucalyptus

Best known for its expectorant properties, the Australian plant eucalyptus is nature's own remedy for respiratory conditions.

Eucalyptus can soothe the mucous membranes, making it a suitable herb for chest infections. It also clears the nasal passages, and has antiseptic properties that are helpful for colds, influenza and sore throats. The essential oil protects from insect bites, and when used as a chest or sinus rub, it has a warming and slightly anaesthetic effect. It may relieve stiffness in rheumatic joints, and help bacterial skin infections.

PROPERTIES/ACTIONS
- Expectorant
- Soothing
- Antiseptic
- Anaesthetic effect

Warning: eucalyptus should not be used by people with liver disorders or digestive problems.

PARTS USED
- Leaves

EUCALYPTUS DECONGESTANT RUB *for colds, blocked noses, etc*

50g (2oz) petroleum jelly
1 tbsp dried lavender
6 drops eucalyptus essential oil
4 drops camphor essential oil
piece of muslin

Melt the petroleum jelly in a bowl over a pan of simmering water. Stir in the lavender and heat for 30 minutes. Strain the jelly through the muslin and leave to cool slightly. Add the oils. Pour into a jar and leave to set. Rub into the chest, throat or back, depending on symptoms.

aloe vera

This herb belongs to the lily family, and its leaves provide a sap that has unique anti-inflammatory and healing properties.

Aloe vera is used most commonly for helping the healing of burns, wounds and skin irritations. When prepared as a juice, it may aid conditions such as colitis, stomach ulcers, kidney stones and constipation. It is rich in nutrients and has been used traditionally for treating everything from fluctuating blood-sugar levels to hangovers. More recently, it has been recognized for its cancer-fighting potential.

PROPERTIES/ACTIONS
- Soothes skin conditions
- Treats digestive problems
- Anti-cancer

PARTS USED
Sap & leaves

Aloe vera was first valued by the ancient Egyptians as a medicinal plant.

ALOE VERA JUICE
for stomach disorders

**5 large aloe vera leaves
piece of muslin**

Pulp the leaves, preferably using a mechanical juicer. Squeeze the pulp through a strainer lined with the muslin to collect the juice. Drink during symptoms.

ginseng (*panax*/Chinese)

Discovered some 5,000 years ago in the mountain provinces of China, *panax ginseng* is a useful nutritive tonic and general stimulant.

Ginseng is well known for its ability to increase energy and vitality. It raises body metabolism and is believed to increase the utilization of nutrients and oxygen in the cells. It also slows the heart rate and decreases the heart's demand for oxygen, and prevents nervous disorders such as anxiety and stress.

Studies show an improvement in cognitive ability with daily usage. Ginseng also treats stomach and digestive troubles, lowers blood-sugar levels and is said to prolong longevity.

PROPERTIES/ACTIONS
- Increases vitality
- Prevents nervous disorders
- Treats digestive troubles
- Aphrodisiac

PARTS USED
- Root

GINSENG SOUP

2 carrots, sliced
2 celery sticks, chopped
2 medium potatoes, peeled
  and chopped
1 onion, chopped
1 tbsp olive oil
4g (⅛oz) dried ginseng root
½ tsp salt
½ tsp black peppercorns
2 litres (70fl oz/8 cups) water

Sweat the vegetables in oil in a large pan for 5–6 minutes. Add the other ingredients. Bring to the boil, then simmer for 2 hours, skimming occasionally. Whizz in a blender. Check the seasoning and serve.

garlic

Originally from Asia, garlic is part of the onion family. It is widely used in cooking, and is an old-fashioned remedy that treats many body systems.

Best known for preventing and treating colds, influenza and sore throats, with anti-viral, antibacterial, anti-microbial and anti-fungal properties, garlic is also useful for bladder and kidney infections, ear infections, and yeast and parasitic infections. It helps arteriosclerosis and high cholesterol, may prevent tumour growth and lowers blood sugar. When eaten raw garlic releases allicin, which has antibiotic effects. It also improves digestion and enhances the absorption of food.

PROPERTIES/ACTIONS
- Good for colds, etc
- Anti-microbial
- Anti-cancer
- Antibiotic effect

PARTS USED
- Bulb

GARLIC COLD SYRUP

1 head of garlic
250ml (8fl oz/1 cup) water
juice of ½ lemon
2 tbsp honey

Crush the garlic cloves, add to water in a saucepan, bring to the boil and simmer for 10 minutes. Add the lemon juice and honey and simmer for a further 2–3 minutes. When cool, strain into a dark glass bottle. Take 2–3 tablespoons 3 times a day. Store in the refrigerator for 2–3 weeks.

090

comfrey

PROPERTIES/ACTIONS
- Heals tissue, bone & cartilage
- Treats skin complaints
Warning: comfrey should not be used internally, or on open wounds.

PARTS USED
- Leaves & root

An ancient wayside plant of the borage family, comfrey is native to Britain and Russia, and is a useful first-aid remedy.

Cultivated since 400BCE, comfrey is one of the most famed healing plants. With the traditional name of "knitbone", it has remarkable powers to heal tissue, bone and cartilage, and was used for these purposes by the Greeks and Romans.

Comfrey's renowned healing ability is due to the presence of a compound called allantoin, which promotes cell proliferation and encourages ligaments and bones to knit together firmly. Allantoin is easily absorbed through the skin, making comfrey a very effective herb for topical use.

COMFREY BRUISE OINTMENT

200g (7oz/⅓ cup) petroleum jelly or paraffin wax
30g (1oz/½ cup) roughly chopped fresh comfrey leaves
piece of muslin

Bring a saucepan of water to the boil. Put the jelly or wax into a glass, heat-proof bowl, and place the bowl over the pan of water. Reduce the heat so that the water is simmering, then add the chopped leaves to the jelly or wax and continue to simmer for about an hour. Remove the bowl from the heat and strain the mixture through the muslin. Pour immediately into a glass jar and allow to set. Use the ointment as needed.

Comfrey has the ability to reduce swellings and can help to heal injuries including fractures. This herb also treats many other skin conditions including psoriasis, eczema and varicose veins, as well as sprains and bruises. Traditionally known as "bruisewort", recent American research has also shown that comfrey breaks down red blood cells, a finding that supports its use for bruises. Comfrey is also valuable in the treatment of scars.

There is some debate on the safety of internal consumption of this herb due to the fact that it contains pyrrolizidine alkaloids which are believed to be toxic to the liver.

Comfrey was known to the ancient Greeks for its amazing ability to make new tissue.

black cohosh

Black cohosh is a Native American remedy long used for women's ailments, especially those associated with menopause.

PROPERTIES/ACTIONS
- Oestrogenic action
- Alleviates menstrual problems
- Benefits rheumatic & arthritic conditions
- Nervine

PARTS USED
- Root

Black cohosh has an oestrogenic action, and is thought to reduce levels of pituitary luteinizing hormone. This makes it useful for alleviating menstrual problems and reducing menopausal hot flushes. Black cohosh also has anti-inflammatory properties, which benefit rheumatic and arthritic conditions. Its expectorant qualities make it useful for asthma and bronchial symptoms. Due to its sedative effect, it can also treat nerve conditions.

BLACK COHOSH DECOCTION

20g (¾oz/⅛ cup) dried or 40g (1½ oz/¼ cup) chopped fresh black cohosh root
750ml (26fl oz/3 cups) water

Place the herb in a saucepan, cover with the water and bring to the boil. Simmer for 20–30 minutes, until the liquid is reduced to about 500ml. Using a sieve, strain the liquid into a jug. Allow to cool or drink hot, taking 50ml 3–4 times a day. Cover the jug and store in the refrigerator for up to 48 hours.

slippery elm

The powdered bark of the elm tree, slippery elm has a long history of use among the Native Americans, who first discovered its distinct strengthening and healing properties.

The mucilage in this herb makes it a soothing remedy for the lining of the stomach, which may help digestive problems such as irritable bowel syndrome, Crohn's disease and colitis. When made into a gruel, it is especially effective for colicky babies. It also soothes sore throats. When used topically, slippery elm disperses inflammation and imparts an emollient effect, thus soothing wounds, burns and itchy, irritated skin.

PROPERTIES/ACTIONS
- Mucilaginous
- Soothes digestive tract
- Eases colic
- Emollient

PARTS USED
- Bark

SLIPPERY ELM SOUP
for the throat & stomach

1 tsp slippery elm powder
1 tsp sugar
455ml (16fl oz/2 cups) boiling water
cinnamon, ginger or nutmeg, to taste

Combine the slippery elm, sugar and water, then mix well. Flavour with the cinnamon, ginger or nutmeg, to taste. Drink as symptoms arise. For a creamier texture, you can use milk instead of water.

- Treats migraine
- Women's herb
- Lowers temperature

PARTS USED
- Leaves

FEVERFEW TINCTURE

200g (7oz/13 cups) dried or 300g (10½oz/19½ cups) chopped fresh feverfew
1 litre (35fl oz/4 cups) alcohol
piece of muslin

Place the herbs and alcohol in a large glass jar. Put the lid on the jar and shake well. Store in a cool, dry place for 10–14 days, shaking the jar every 1–2 days. Strain the herbs from the liquid by pouring it through the piece of muslin. Discard the herbs. Pour the tincture into a dark glass bottle with a lid. Take 5 drops with water up to 3 times a day.

feverfew

Feverfew is now used principally as a treatment for migraine, but has long been thought of as a herb for a variety of other ailments.

Although the exact nature of its actions is not yet fully understood, the constituent parthenolide found in feverfew appears to inhibit the release of the hormone serotonin, which is thought to trigger migraine.

Feverfew also has many gynaecological uses for women. With a stimulant effect on the uterus, it can induce menstruation, and with relaxant and analgesic properties it eases period pains. Feverfew can lower temperature and has traditionally been used for hot flushes during menopause.

horseradish

Horseradish is traditionally used as a condiment, to aid the digestion of roasted meats. It also has a long history in ancient medical circles.

Horseradish stimulates gastric secretions, acting as a general digestive aid. With its natural siligrin content, it has powerful antibacterial, antibiotic and even anti-cancer properties. Horseradish is also a good diuretic and promotes perspiration, making it useful for fevers, colds and influenza.

Because of its expectorant qualities, the herb is used for upper respiratory tract disorders, especially sinus troubles. It is anti-spasmodic and acts as a circulatory stimulant, and may help arthritis, gout and rheumatism.

PROPERTIES/ACTIONS
- Antibiotic action
- Anti-cancer
- Diuretic
- Treats sinus troubles
- Anti-spasmodic

PARTS USED
- Root

HORSERADISH TEA

1 tsp peeled and grated horseradish root
250ml (8fl oz/1 cup) water
1 tsp honey

Pour the water into a saucepan and bring to the boil. Drop the horseradish root into the boiling water. Reduce the heat and leave to simmer for 2 minutes, then strain. Pour the infusion into a cup and add honey to taste.

elderflower

PROPERTIES/ACTIONS
- Immuno-stimulant
- Induces sweating
- Diuretic
- Treats respiratory conditions

PARTS USED
- Flowers & berries

Traditionally known as "nature's medicine chest
the elder tree provides both flowers and berries
with medicinal properties.

Elderflower has a well-established reputation as an imm
stimulant and for fighting coughs and colds. It can inc
perspiration, and is useful in the treatment of fevers. By ac
as a diuretic, elder flowering tops aid the removal of w
products and are valuable in arthritic conditions. They also
the mucous linings of the nose and throat, increas
resistance to conditions such as asthma, bronchitis, sinu
and hayfever. Elderflowers contain ursolic acid, which has
anti-inflammatory action and can soothe chapped skin.

ELDERFLOWER SALVE
for dry, chapped skin

150g (5½oz) emulsifying wax
70g (2½oz) glycerine
80ml (2½fl oz/⅓ cup) water
30g (1oz) dried or 75g (2½oz)
fresh elderflower tops

Melt the wax in a glass bowl
set in a pan of boiling water.
Stir in the glycerine, water and
herbs. Simmer for 3 hours.
Strain through a muslin-lined
strainer. Stir until cool and set.
Transfer to dark glass jars with
lids. Rub into the affected area
3 times a day. Store in the
refrigerator for up to 3 months.

thyme

With its pungent scent, thyme has been used by healers for centuries, and today is among the most common and useful of herbs in the garden.

A stimulating herb, thyme works well as a tonic for the nerves, helping to combat mental stress and enhance mood. It has powerful antiseptic, antibacterial and anti-viral actions, and is used for treating respiratory troubles such as asthma, coughs and colds, and allergic reactions. With a local anaesthetic-like effect, thyme has proved useful for tonsillitis. Applied topically, thyme can help heal wounds as well as muscular pain. Thyme also contains strong anti-fungal properties for treating nail fungus, athlete's foot and yeast infections.

PROPERTIES/ACTIONS
- Nervine tonic
- Treats respiratory conditions
- Anaesthetic-like action
- Anti-fungal

PARTS USED
- Leaves

THYME LINCTUS
for disorders of the respiratory tract

25g (1oz) fresh thyme leaves
25g (1oz) fresh borage
 flowers and leaves
2 small cinnamon sticks
455ml (16fl oz/2 cups) water
juice of 1 small lemon
100g (4oz) honey

Simmer the herbs and cinnamon in a saucepan of water for 20 minutes. Strain, and return the liquid to the pan. Simmer until reduced by half. Add the lemon juice and honey; simmer for 5 minutes. Take 1 teaspoon as required.

PROPERTIES/ACTIONS
- Nourishing
- Rich in iron
- Dense in chlorophyll

PARTS USED
- Leaves

NETTLE TONIC TEA

1 litre (35fl oz/4 cups) water
40–50g (1½–2oz/½–1 cup)
chopped nettle leaves

Put the water in a saucepan
and bring to the boil. Add the
nettle leaves to the water.
Reduce the heat and simmer
for 5–10 minutes. Strain and
discard the herbs. Drink 1 cup
3 times a day before meals.

nettle

Stinging nettle nourishes the whole system,
specifically the adrenals and kidneys, and has
long been used as a remedy for rheumatism.

Very high in iron, nettle is a good tonic for blood disorders
such as anaemia. The leaves are high in chlorophyll, which acts
on the hormonal system, and the root is rich in vitamin C,
which boosts immunity and treats conditions such as hayfever.

Nettle is often used to reduce inflammation in allergic
responses and rheumatism. It is also a nourishing tonic for
pregnant and lactating women.

hawthorn

Part of the rose family, hawthorn came to the attention of the medical profession in the 1890s and became known as the herb for "hearts".

The hawthorn plant has a vasodilatory effect, proving an excellent remedy for high blood pressure and angina. Hawthorn also acts on the vagus nerve, treating mild arrthymia. By increasing circulation to the brain, hawthorn improves memory. It also decreases inflammation caused by allergies, and has a relaxant effect in the digestive tract, relieving intestinal discomfort.

PROPERTIES/ACTIONS
- Vasodilator
- Improves memory
- Relaxes digestive tract
- Treats nervous conditions

PARTS USED
- Flowers & berries

HAWTHORN "HEART" TINCTURE

200g (7oz/1 cup) dried or 300g (10½oz/1½ cups) chopped fresh hawthorn flowers or berries
1 litre (35fl oz/4 cups) alcohol
piece of muslin

Place the hawthorn in a large glass jar and cover with the alcohol. Secure the lid and shake. Store in a cool, dark place for 10–14 days, shaking every 1 or 2 days. Strain through the muslin into a dark glass bottle. Take 1 teaspoon 3 times a day in 25ml water or juice. Store for up to 2 years.

St John's wort

Historically, St John's wort has been used for a number of disorders, but it is best known for its treatment of mild depression.

PROPERTIES/ACTIONS
- Anti-depressant
- Fights colds
- Treats nervous system
- Astringent

PARTS USED
- Flowers

This herb is said to lend a sunny disposition and is used for depression, anxiety and fatigue, as well as loss of appetite. It is a powerful anti-viral and fights colds, herpes simplex and hepatitis. It is also traditionally used for affections of the nervous system, namely neuralgia and sciatica. As an astringent and diuretic it is useful for inflammatory conditions, particularly those of the urinary tract.

OIL INFUSION
for inflammatory skin conditions

1 handful fresh or dried St John's wort flowers
500ml (16fl oz/2 cups) olive oil

Place the herbs in a glass bottle or jar with a stopper, and cover with the olive oil. Drizzle the oil on salads, removing any flowers. Steep until all the oil is used.

chicory

Wild chicory enjoys a reputation in traditional medicine as a great spring tonic with powerful cleansing and detoxifying abilities.

Chicory leaves, commonly used in salads, are effective as a liver stimulant. With an amazing ability to promote secretion of bile, chicory treats jaundice and aids the detoxifying process.

Chicory has an equally beneficial effect on the kidneys, and is useful for urinary infections, skin problems, arthritis, rheumatism and gout. It also has anti-inflammatory properties and can settle stomach disorders.

PROPERTIES/ACTIONS
• Liver stimulant
• Good for skin problems
• Helps arthritis
• Settles the stomach

PARTS USED
• Root & leaves

OLD-FASHIONED CHICORY DEPURATIVE SYRUP

1 kg (2lb 4oz/6 cups) fresh chicory root
500g (1lb 2oz/2½ cups) granulated sugar

Wash the chicory root thoroughly, then press through a juicer. Place the juice in a saucepan together with the sugar. Bring to the boil, then reduce the heat and simmer for about 20 minutes, until the juice acquires a syrupy consistency. Store in a tightly sealed bottle. Take 1 teaspoon 1–3 times a day.

lavender

This fragrant herb, which adorns our gardens in the spring and has been popular since the Middle Ages, is a unique tonic for the nervous system.

Lavender is a tonic and sedative, and may therefore help anxiety, headaches, insomnia and general stress. It also has antibacterial and antiseptic properties, useful for conditions such as acne, eczema and yeast infections.

Due to its antihistamine properties, inhaling the vapours of lavender essential oil is useful in treating bronchitis, and lavender's prostaglandin-inhibiting effects can help to reduce the pain and swelling of burns and bites. Lavender is also anti-spasmodic and a diuretic.

PROPERTIES/ACTIONS
- Soothing
- Treats anxiety & insomnia
- Antihistamine effect

PARTS USED
- Whole herb

LAVENDER COMPRESS
for headaches, burns, bites, etc

15g (½oz/¼ cup) dried or 30g (1oz/½ cup) fresh lavender
250ml (8fl oz/1 cup) vodka
50ml (2fl oz/¼ cup) water
piece of paper towel
square of cotton cloth

Put the herb in a glass jar with the vodka and water. Cover and leave in a cool, dark place for 7–10 days. Strain off the lavender with a sieve lined with a paper towel, and wrap it in the cloth. Apply directly to the affected area. Alternatively, make a liniment by soaking a cotton-wool pad in the tincture and dabbing it onto the skin.

chamomile

One of the herbs in the Anglo-Saxon "Nine Herbs Charm", chamomile has an ancient and detailed medicinal history.

Chamomile is best known for its calming nervine effects and is often used to treat anxiety and insomnia, as well as attention deficit hyperactivity disorder (ADHD). It is also an antihistamine, thus relieving allergic symptoms, and has anti-inflammatory and anti-spasmodic properties that help it to treat digestive disorders such as irritable bowel syndrome, as well as PMS and skin conditions such as eczema.

Chamomile is an excellent remedy for children's ailments, including colic and teething.

PROPERTIES/ACTIONS
- Carminative
- Sedative
- Antihistamine
- Anti-spasmodic
- Children's remedy

PARTS USED
- Whole herb

STEAM INHALATION
for problematic skin

½ **tsp chopped chamomile leaves**
250ml (8fl oz/1 cup) purified water

Simmer the herbs and water in a saucepan for 30 minutes. Pour the boiling water and herbs into a bowl and, keeping your face within a safe distance from the water, cover both your head and the bowl with a towel and inhale for about 30 seconds. Repeat 2 or 3 times a day.

chickweed

Although the active constituents in chickweed are largely unknown, it is a renowned folk remedy for a number of conditions.

With its demulcent and cooling properties, chickweed is especially useful for the treatment of conditions such as eczema, nappy rash, and even chicken pox. When applied as a compress, it can treat conjunctivitis and ear infections.

Traditional Chinese herbalists use chickweed to treat everything from asthma and indigestion, to nosebleeds and rheumatic conditions.

PROPERTIES/ACTIONS
- Demulcent
- Cooling
- Soothes skin

PARTS USED
- Whole herb

CHICKWEED OIL
for skin & rheumatic conditions

375g (13oz/6 cups) fresh chickweed (leaves and flowers)
225ml (8fl oz/1 cup) sunflower oil

Pour the sunflower oil into a bowl and place it over a large saucepan of boiling water. Add the chickweed. Simmer gently for 2 hours, topping up the water as necessary. Strain the oil into a bottle. Dab the oil directly onto the skin. Alternatively, add 1 tablespoon to warm bath water.

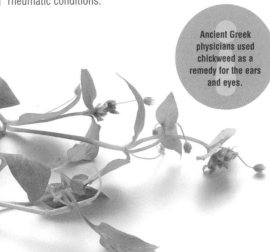

Ancient Greek physicians used chickweed as a remedy for the ears and eyes.

tea tree

Native to Australia, tea tree is part of the clove family and provides one of the most effective natural antiseptics.

With its antibacterial, anti-fungal and renowned antiseptic properties, tea tree is an effective remedy for a broad range of conditions, especially fungal and skin problems like ringworm, insects bites and stings, acne, athlete's foot and yeast infections. Tea tree is effective as a mouthwash, counteracting gum disease, and can also be used as a gargle for sore throats. It is useful as a remedy for coughs and colds.

PROPERTIES/ACTIONS
• Anti-fungal
• Antiseptic
• Treats skin infections
• Useful for oral infections

PARTS USED
• Leaves

TEA TREE SKIN WASH

1 tsp dried or 2 tsp fresh tea tree leaves
250ml (8fl oz/1 cup) water, freshly boiled

Steep the herbs in the water for 5–10 minutes, then strain. Allow to cool, then bathe the skin or affected area. Repeat when required.

lemon balm

With a lovely citrus scent, lemon balm has many medicinal, culinary and aromatic uses.

Due to its sedating effects, lemon balm has been used traditionally for treating menstrual cramps and headaches, healing wounds, easing digestion, preventing insomnia and relaxing the nerves. It stimulates the liver and gallbladder, and enhances digestion and absorption. The herb has a particular affinity for easing nausea, colitis, colic and irritable bowel syndrome. It has antibacterial, anti-viral and mucus-reducing properties, and is good for children's coughs and colds. Used topically, it can relieve swellings, bruises, bites and cold sores.

PROPERTIES/ACTIONS
- Sedating
- Liver & gallbladder stimulant
- Treats digestive conditions
- Reduces mucus

PARTS USED
- Whole herb

LEMON BALM SALVE
for bruises, bites & cold sores

handful of lemon balm leaves, dried or fresh
250ml (8fl oz/1 cup) almond oil
25g (1oz) beeswax
½ tbsp vitamin E oil
piece of muslin

Place the herbs in a glass jar and cover with the almond oil. Leave for 2 weeks, shaking daily, then strain through the muslin. Melt the beeswax in a pan. Add the oil and mix. Off the heat, add the vitamin E oil. Store in jars in the refrigerator. Apply liberally to the skin.

cinnamon

With a long history of use in India, cinnamon is now one of the world's most important spices, with a plethora of healing properties.

Stimulating and warming, cinnamon is a traditional remedy for digestive problems such as nausea, vomiting and diarrhoea, as well as for aching muscles and other symptoms of viral conditions such as colds and influenza. Due to its heating properties, it can promote sweating, thus helping to lower body temperature during fever. It can also be used for treating mild food poisoning, and is good for bleeding gums and used as a mouthwash for halitosis.

In the Middle Ages cinnamon was used as a flavouring as well as for its curative powers.

PROPERTIES/ACTIONS
- Warming stimulant
- Carminative
- Anti-spasmodic
- Antiseptic
- Anti-viral

PARTS USED
- Inner bark & twigs

CINNAMON TEA
for colds & fevers

1 heaped tsp ground cinnamon
honey, to taste

Put the ground cinnamon into a cup and pour over boiling water. Leave to infuse for 5 minutes, then strain through a sieve. Sweeten with honey to taste. Take 1–2 cups within 2 hours.

ginger

PROPERTIES/ACTIONS
- Anti-nausea
- Carminitive
- Circulatory stimulant
- Boosts immunity
- Inhibits coughing

PARTS USED
- Root

Thought to have derived from the Garden of Eden, ginger is a favourite spice and flavouring, and one of the world's greatest medicines.

Used in India and China since 5000 BC, ginger is grown throughout the tropics and used extensively as both a culinary and therapeutic spice. It contains an active constituent, gingerol, which is responsible for much of its hot, pungent taste and aroma, as well as its stimulating properties.

Ginger's volatile oil also lends many medicinal effects, working on the digestive system by encouraging secretion of digestive enzymes. Ginger is a wonderful remedy for indigestion, wind and colic. It invigorates the stomach and intestines, and relieves complaints such as motion and morning sickness. Moving stagnation of food and

---

GINGER & LEMON SORE THROAT DECOCTION

115g (4oz) piece of fresh root ginger
500ml (17fl oz/2¼ cups) water
zest and juice of 1 lemon
pinch of cayenne pepper

Slice the ginger (there is no need to peel it) and put it in a saucepan together with the water, lemon zest and cayenne pepper. Bring to the boil, cover the pan and simmer for

20 minutes. Remove from the heat and add the lemon juice. Drink 1 cup according to symptoms. The decoction will keep for 2–3 days.

accumulation of toxins, including fungal infections, ginger increases vitality and enhances immunity.

Additionally, ginger is warming and soothing, and is a favourite home remedy for colds and influenza. It promotes perspiration, reducing a fever and clearing congestion, and has a stimulating and expectorant action in the lungs, expelling phlegm and relieving coughs. Ginger is also a useful remedy for pain and inflammation, helping cramps, peptic ulcers, allergies and asthma. It has a stimulating effect on the circulation, lowering high blood pressure.

The Roman Apicius included ginger in many recipes for sweet and savoury sauces.

turmeric

Grown for its root, turmeric is the most common flavour and colour present in Far Eastern cooking, and the root has a host of medicinal properties.

Turmeric is used in traditional Chinese medicine to treat the liver and gallbladder. It is a useful remedy that may help everything from gallstones and jaundice, to premenstrual discomfort and skin conditions.

The spice is known to have effective anti-inflammatory and analgesic properties, good for treating arthritic and rheumatic problems as well as digestive disorders. Turmeric is high in antioxidants and due to its active ingredient, curcumin, has antibacterial and even cancer-fighting potential. It is an anti-coagulant, and has cholesterol-lowering properties.

TURMERIC POULTICE
for skin inflammation

**fresh piece of turmeric root
gauze bandage**

Grind the turmeric in a food processor to make a powder. Mix 1 teaspoon with a little water to make a paste. Wrap the paste in a bandage and tie to the affected area. Leave for 20 minutes, then discard. Repeat 3 times a day.

cayenne pepper

A fiery spice, cayenne pepper was first introduced to the West in the 16th century. It is a finely ground variety of chilli, with similar properties.

Cayenne, with the active constituent capsaicin, is a warming stimulant and a remedy for poor circulation. Applied to the skin, capsaicin desensitizes nerve endings and acts as a counter-irritant, helping local blood flow.

It may help psoriasis, neuralgia, headaches and arthritis. Cayenne is taken to relieve wind and colic and to stimulate secretion of the digestive juices, as well as to aid metabolism.

The name "cayenne" derives from that of a French Guianan town of the same name.

PROPERTIES/ACTIONS
- Stimulant
- Improves circulation
- Treats wind & colic
- Aids metabolism

PARTS USED
- Fresh & dried pepper

CAYENNE-INFUSED OIL
for the skin

**100g (3½oz/⅝ cup) finely chopped cayenne pepper
500ml (17fl oz/2¼ cups) vegetable or olive oil**

Place the cayenne and oil in a heat-proof bowl. Bring a large saucepan of water to the boil, then reduce the heat and simmer gently. Set the bowl over the saucepan and leave for 2–3 hours. Remove from the heat and allow to cool. Strain the infused oil, using a funnel, into a dark glass bottle. Apply to the skin when needed.

080

anise

Used for centuries as a folk medicine as well as a spice, anise seed and its fruit, star anise, have similar therapeutic properties.

Anise seed is a good remedy to ease griping, intestinal colic and flatulence. It has marked expectorant action and may be used for bronchitis and for persistent, irritable coughing. With mild oestrogenic effects, anise seed can be used to increase milk secretion in lactating women. The fruit of the anise plant, known as star anise, has a similar effect, but with its ability to relieve muscle spasms, it is also used in herbal remedies for rheumatism, back pain and hernias. Star anise is also used for toothache. Both the seed and the fruit act as a heart stimulant.

PROPERTIES/ACTIONS
- Stimulant
- Oestrogenic
- Relieves muscle spasm

PARTS USED
- Seed & fruit

HONEYED PEARS WITH ANISEED *for coughs*

½ tsp aniseed
1 pear, cored and sliced
1 dry fig
1 date
1 tsp honey

Place all the ingredients in a small saucepan. Cover and simmer gently for 45 minutes, or until the fruit is soft. Remove from the heat and eat immediately.

nutmeg

Nutmeg has been an important part of the spice trade since the 6th century. It has also long been valued for its effect on the digestive system.

Nutmeg has a natural stimulating and anaesthetic effect on the stomach and intestines, and may help to reduce nausea and vomiting. It can also be a helpful remedy for gastroenteritis, and is excellent for treating diarrhoea, helping to warm the intestines and relieve abdominal pain.

In Ayurvedic medicine, nutmeg is a remedy for insomnia and coughs, and is believed to promote healthy skin. With a counter-irritant effect, it stimulates blood flow, helping to treat rheumatic conditions and eczema.

PROPERTIES/ACTIONS
- Stimulant
- Reduces nausea
- Helps diarrhoea
- Promotes healthy skin

PARTS USED
- Seed

SPICED NUTMEG SALVE
for rheumatism & inflammed skin

50g (2oz) petroleum jelly
1 tsp coarsley grated nutmeg
6 drops neroli essential oil
piece of muslin

Melt the jelly in a bowl over a pan of simmering water. Stir in the nutmeg and leave for 30 minutes. Strain through the muslin, leave to cool slightly, then add the essential oil. Pour into a glass jar and leave until set. Use as needed.

sprouts

First discovered by Chinese physicians more than 5,000 years ago, sprouts are full of all kinds of health-promoting enzymes, nutrients and sugars.

PROPERTIES/ACTIONS
- Rich in enzymes
- Dense in nutrients
- Highly digestible
- Anti-cancer

PARTS USED
- Whole sprout

As a seed, sprouts' powerful enzymes that otherwise lie dormant are released. The starches within seeds are also converted into natural sugars. Sprouts are easily digested and assimilated, and provide more nutrients gram for gram than any other natural food known. They help every cell in the body to function efficiently. Because sprouts are generally high in vitamin C, they are useful in boosting immunity. Some sprouts are believed to have anti-cancer properties.

SPROUT SALAD

200g (7oz/2 cups) mung bean sprouts
200g (7oz/2 cups) alfalfa sprouts
50g (2oz/¼ cup) fenugreek sprouts
1 medium lettuce, finely chopped
50g (2oz/¼ cup) finely chopped sunflower greens (baby plants from unhulled seeds grown in soil)
favourite salad dressing, to taste

Put all the salad vegetables in a bowl. Season with the salad dressing. Toss and serve.

seaweed

Seaweed is a marine algae, the oldest form of life on the planet, and it contains a host of health-giving properties, particularly minerals.

Seaweed is rich in minerals such as potassium, magnesium, calcium and iron, as well as trace elements, and benefits many body systems. Due to its high iodine content, it aids digestion and soothes ulcers. It also promotes the functioning of the thyroid and metabolism. Seaweed is filled with mucilaginous gels that alkalinize the blood, treating rheumatic complaints. It also helps clear liver stagnation, treating PMS, headaches and skin problems. Seaweed is an excellent lymphatic cleanser.

PROPERTIES/ACTIONS
- High in iodine
- Supports thyroid & metabolism
- Mucilaginous
- Clears liver stagnation
- Lymphatic cleanser

PARTS USED
- Whole plant

SEAWEED RICE

2 tbsp wakame
625ml (20fl oz/2½ cups) warm water
½ medium onion, chopped
2 large garlic cloves, minced
200g (7oz/1 cup) brown rice

Rinse the wakame, and soak in the warm water for 5 minutes. Squeeze dry and chop. Save the water and heat 1 tablespoon in a pan. Sauté the onion gently for 2 minutes, stirring. Add all the other ingredients and the remaining water. Bring to the boil, then simmer for 35 minutes. Serve.

wheatgrass

PROPERTIES/ACTIONS
- Dense in nutrients
- Nourishing
- High in protein
- Rich in chlorophyll
- Purifies & rebuilds
- Antiseptic

PARTS USED
- Grass blades

An ancient biblical manuscript describes wheatgrass as the perfect food.

Identified during the 1930s as a complete food, this young cereal grass is now recognized as one of nature's great superfoods.

Fresh wheatgrass contains many enzymes and amino acids, as well as all the B-group vitamins, vitamins A, C, E and K, and calcium, magnesium, manganese, phosphorus, potassium, zinc and selenium. Wheatgrass contains up to 40 percent protein, making it valuable in the healing process.

The solid content of wheatgrass consists of 70 percent chlorophyll, which closely resembles the molecules of haemoglobin. It increases the functions of the heart, and improves the vascular system, the intestines, the uterus and the lungs. Chlorophyll is also good for anaemia, and has a dilating effect on the blood vessels, therefore reducing high blood pressure. It is a powerful antioxidant, making it a

WHEATGRASS POULTICE

1 tray fresh wheatgrass
cotton-wool pad
gauze bandage

Juice 2 handfuls of wheatgrass (as described opposite), then soak the cotton-wool pad in the juice. Squeeze out any excess juice, then apply the cotton-wool pad to the

affected area and secure with the gauze bandage. Leave for 20 minutes, then discard. Apply the poultice as necessary, up to 3 times a day.

fantastic detoxifier. In addition, chlorophyll has the ability to heal infected and ulcerated wounds, as well as common skin conditions. It has antiseptic properties, and is effective in healing bleeding gums, ulcers, gingivitis and sore throats.

WHEATGRASS JUICE

**1 tray fresh wheatgrass
masticating juicer**

To harvest the wheatgrass, grasp a small bundle of the growing blades firmly, then, using a sharp knife, cut them off above the compost level. Rinse in cold water and feed into the masticating juicer while it is in motion. Push the wheatgrass down until juice appears. Repeat with 2 or 3 bundles. Drink 2 tablespoons each day.

lamb

PROPERTIES/ACTIONS
- Rich in protein
- Prevents anaemia
- Boosts immunity
- Improves circulation

PARTS USED
- Lamb

As well as being a traditional symbol of continuing life and resurrection, lamb has valuable nutritious properties.

Like other red meat, lamb is rich in protein, as well as being an excellent source of two vital minerals: iron and zinc. Iron helps to boost the oxygen-carrying capability of blood, preventing anaemia and fatigue from setting in, while zinc is necessary for optimum functioning of the immune system, helping to fight colds, infections and other invaders.

According to the Chinese eating lamb improves circulation, overcomes coldness, and may even treat post-natal depression.

LAMB KOFTA

450g (1lb) finely ground lamb
1 large onion, grated
1 tsp salt
30g (1oz/1 cup) finely
  chopped fresh parsley
¼ tsp black pepper
1 tsp ground allspice

Combine the ingredients and chill for 1 hour. Divide and shape into balls, then thread the balls onto a skewer. Cook under the grill until browned on all sides.

beef

Reserved in Britain for the ruling Normans until after the 13th century, beef is a flavourful meat with many therapeutic attributes.

A rich source of animal protein, beef has high levels of iron, zinc and many B-complex vitamins, and may help to protect against chronic fatigue syndrome, anaemia, weak digestion, depression and mood swings. According to the Chinese eating beef lifts body metabolism, treats hypoglycaemia and strengthens bones. Organic beef is free from pesticides and contains conjugated linoleic acid, which has cancer-fighting properties and stimulates the conversion of stored fat into energy.

PROPERTIES/ACTIONS
- Rich in iron, zinc & B vitamins
- Prevents anaemia
- Good for mood swings

PARTS USED
- Beef

PEPPER STEAKS

4 beef fillet steaks
2 tbsp olive oil
6 tbsp assorted cracked
   peppercorns
2 garlic cloves, crushed
40g (1½oz) butter
salt and pepper, to taste

Coat the steaks with the olive oil. Press down on the peppercorns, then press them into the steaks. Coat the steaks thoroughly with the crushed garlic. Melt the butter in a large frying pan. Cook the steaks over a medium heat for 3–4 minutes on each side. Season to taste with the salt and pepper.

salmon

Containing a wealth of omega-3 fatty acids and other health-giving properties, salmon is essential to the diet.

PROPERTIES/ACTIONS
- Rich in omega-3 fatty acids
- Good for skin
- Promotes healthy nervous system
- Treats behavioural problems

PARTS USED
- Salmon

> The deeper the colour of salmon, the more beneficial omega-3 fatty acids it contains.

Salmon is a source of protein, minerals and B vitamins. Being high in omega-3 it regulates immune-boosting white blood cells, prevents high blood pressure, lowers blood cholesterol, may help conditions of the central nervous system, reduces inflammation and could even help fight against cancer. It is especially good for arthritis and skin conditions such as psoriasis and eczema.

SIZZLING SALMON

500g/(1lb 2oz) salmon fillet
½ tsp crushed dried chillies
¼ tsp paprika
4 tsp olive oil
salt and pepper, to taste
4 tsp chopped coriander leaves

Cut the salmon into four. Place skin-side down on a griddle pan and sprinkle with the chillies, paprika and oil. Season with salt and pepper, and cook for 6–8 minutes. Place the salmon on four serving plates and sprinkle with the chopped coriander. Serve immediately.

prawn

Prawns belong to an animal group called crustaceans, and they provide top-quality, easily digested protein, along with many other nutrients.

Prawns are rich in antioxidants, zinc and selenium, which help to fight colds and infection, promote a healthy heart and offer protection against prostate and breast cancer. They are high in vitamin B12, which is crucial to red blood cells. They also supply iodine, necessary for a healthy thyroid, calcium for strong bones, and omega-3 fatty acids for skin and hormonal health.

Prawns bought with the shells left on have a better flavour than those already shelled.

PROPERTIES/ACTIONS
- High in zinc & selenium
- Rich in vitamin B12
- Good for thyroid

PARTS USED
- Whole prawn, peeled

CARIBBEAN PRAWNS

**1 tsp each ground cinnamon and cumin, red chilli, curry powder, cayenne, black pepper, salt and allspice
600g (1lb 5oz/5 cups) large prawns, peeled and cleaned**

Preheat the oven to 200°C/400°F/Gas Mark 6. Combine the spices in a bowl. Use the mixed spices to coat the prawns. In a frying pan, sear the prawns for a crust-like coating. Place in a baking dish and bake for about 10 minutes. Serve hot on wild rice and top with citrus salsa.

oyster

Oysters are bisexual, or inter-sexual, changing from males to females.

Oysters are a type of shellfish that is not only a renowned aphrodisiac, but also full of health-promoting vitamins, minerals and other nutrients.

Oysters are an excellent source of protein. They are rich in vitamin E and omega-3 fatty acids for heart health, and have many brain-boosting B vitamins, including B12, which helps fight fatigue. They also contain vitamin D, which is needed for healthy bones and teeth, as well as potassium, iron and selenium. In Chinese medicine, they supplement the liver and kidneys, and treat insomnia, restlessness and agitation.

Oysters have a well-documented affinity with the reproductive system. They are a rich source of iodine, which is

OYSTERS AU PARMESAN

125g (4½oz/1 cup) breadcrumbs
1 tbsp butter
3 dozen fresh oysters
salt and cayenne pepper
15g (½oz/½ cup) chopped fesh parsley
125g (4½oz/1 cup) freshly grated Parmesan cheese

125ml (4fl oz/½ cup) white wine

Preheat the oven to 180°C/350°F/Gas Mark 4. In a pan, brown the breadcrumbs in the butter, reserving 1 tablespoon. Grease a shallow baking dish, then dust with the fried breadcrumbs. Season the

oysters with salt and cayenne pepper and place them on top of the breadcrumbs. Scatter the parsley and Parmesan cheese on top, followed by the remaining breadcrumbs. Pour the wine over the entire dish. Bake in the oven for 15 minutes. Serve hot.

necessary for the proper functioning of the thyroid and the reproductive hormones. Research also indicates that certain sterols are present in oysters, from which the sex hormones are derived. They are used regularly by Chinese women to increase oestrogen in the body, and are useful for infertility and for treating menopausal disorders. Oysters are a rich natural source of nutrients, including zinc – just six raw oysters provide excellent amounts of this important nutrient. Zinc is essential for the production of sperm and enhances libido. It also helps to boost immunity.

chicken

Discovered by the ancient Egyptians in the 14th century BC, chicken has become an everyday food with health-giving properties.

In addition to protein, chicken is a good source of B-complex vitamins and is rich in absorbable iron and zinc – with twice as much in the dark meat as in the breast – thus fighting anaemia and boosting immunity. The breast contains double the amount of vitamin B6, which fights PMS. Chicken promotes circulation and invigorates the kidneys, thus treating diarrhoea and oedema. Made into a soup, chicken is known to be soothing and restorative. Chicken soup is an effective remedy for colds and infections of the upper respiratory tract.

PROPERTIES/ACTIONS
- Fights anaemia
- Boosts immunity
- Rich in vitamin B6
- Promotes circulation
- Soothing

PARTS USED
- Chicken

GRANDMA'S CHICKEN SOUP

225g (8oz) skinless, boneless chicken breast, cubed
2¼ litres/79fl oz/9 cups) chicken broth
6 garlic cloves, minced
1 medium piece fresh ginger, cut into 2 or 3 chunks
4 spring onions, chopped

Bring the broth, garlic and ginger to the boil in a pan, then simmer for 10 minutes. Add the chicken and cook for 5–7 minutes. Discard the ginger. Top with the onions to serve.

Choose organic chicken; intensively farmed birds contain harmful pesticides.

milk

Milk is soothing and comforting, and provides liquid nutrition that is helpful in preventing and treating a great many conditions.

Milk is a first-class protein, providing building blocks that are especially useful in a child's diet. It is a rich source of calcium, which strengthens the bones and prevents osteoporosis, as well as some B vitamins, iron and zinc. Some studies show that milk may be good for the brain and for preventing strokes. It may contain substances that reduce the liver's production of cholesterol and lower blood pressure.

Irish folk medicine states that sheep droppings were given in milk for whooping cough.

PROPERTIES/ACTIONS
- First-class protein
- Rich in calcium
- Strengthens bones

PARTS USED
- Milk

MILK & HONEY BATH LOTION *to nourish the skin*

150ml (5fl oz/⅔ cup) milk
2 eggs
3 tbsp carrier oil
2 tsp honey
2 tsp organic shampoo
1 tbsp vodka

In a bowl, beat together the eggs and oil. Add the other ingredients, mix and pour into a glass bottle. Add 30–45ml (1–1½fl oz) to bath water. Keep the remaining lotion chilled and use within 3–4 days.

yoghurt

PROPERTIES/ACTIONS
- Contains "friendly" bacteria
- Fights infections
- Helps stomach ulcers
- Rich in calcium

PARTS USED
- Fermented milk

Ancient Bedouins discovered that heat and movement fermented the milk to create yoghurt.

A cultured milk product, yoghurt is positively brimming with "friendly" bacteria and many health-promoting nutrients.

Containing live cultures such as *Lactobacillus* and *Bifida* bacteria, yoghurt stimulates the production of anti-viral and antibacterial agents and helps to fight off infections. These "friendly" bacteria attack and destroy the "bad" bacteria that cause food poisoning, as well as allowing the gut to absorb other essential nutrients efficiently.

The bacteria synthesize B vitamins, biotin, folic acid and vitamin B12, which helps fight depression, and increase the absorption of calcium and magnesium needed for healthy bones. Yoghurt also supplies small traces of vitamin D, which is essential for the absorption of calcium.

YOGHURT & EVENING PRIMROSE FACE MASK *for revitalizing & replenishing tired skin*

2 capsules evening primrose oil
3 tbsp live yoghurt
1 tsp honey
2 capsules vitamin E oil
30g (1oz) potato flour

Extract the oil from the evening primrose oil capsules and combine it in a bowl with the other ingredients. Add extra flour to achieve the desired consistency.

Apply the mask evenly to the face and leave for approximately 20 minutes. Wash off with water and pat dry. Repeat the process each evening, as desired.

Yoghurt is especially useful for preventing yeast infections that cause itching, burning and other uncomfortable symptoms, and offers some relief from stomach ulcers. It may also help to prevent cancer. Some studies have found that the probiotics present in yoghurt produce enzymes that are absorbed directly through the gut wall, which further strengthens immune defences. Yoghurt also provides an alternative for those who cannot tolerate the lactose in milk.

LASSI
South Indian yoghurt drink

250g (9oz/1 cup) plain yoghurt
625ml(21fl oz/2½ cups) cold
  water
1 tsp cumin seeds
½ tsp salt
½ tsp finely chopped fresh
  mint

Put all the ingredients in a blender and whizz for a few seconds, until well mixed. Serve cold.

coffee

Coffee first arrived in Europe from Arabia in the 1600s, when it was valued as a medicine, and has since evolved as a popular beverage.

Containing caffeine, coffee is a proven pick-me-up that stimulates the brain and improves mental performance and concentration. It can also bolster mood and mild depression. With its ability to relax the bronchial muscles, coffee is helpful to some asthmatics. It can also offer relief from migraine.

Coffee is a diuretic and can therefore relieve constipation. It may also help to prevent cancer. A poultice of wet coffee grounds can speed the healing of insect bites and bruises.

PROPERTIES/ACTIONS
- Brain stimulant
- Treats asthma
- Diuretic
- Purgative

PARTS USED
- Beans

COFFEE POULTICE
for insect bites & bruises

50g (1¾oz/⅓ cup) coffee grounds
60ml (2fl oz/¼ cup) water
gauze bandage

Soak the coffee in the water, then spread directly onto the affected area. Cover and wrap with the gauze bandage. Leave for several hours, or until the coffee dries.

094

tea

The most popular beverage in the world, tea is refreshing and nutritive. It is also used therapeutically in many traditional cultures.

Tea contains useful quantities of nutrients like vitamins E and K for the skin and blood, manganese for growth and the function of hormones, and fluorine for protection against tooth decay. In small quantities, the astringent tannins are antibacterial and can help with stomach infections. Green tea is particularly rich in bioflavonoids, which help to fend off damaging free radicals.

Externally, the tannins and antioxidants can be utilized by placing tea bags over sticky, itchy or tired eyes.

PROPERTIES/ACTIONS
- Nutritive
- Astringent
- Fights free radicals

PARTS USED
- Leaves

Tea ceremonies are held in China and Japan to celebrate the healing properties of tea.

BLACK TEA EYE SOAK

2 black tea bags
60ml (l4fl oz/¼ cup) water

Place the tea bags in a small bowl and allow them to mop up the water. Wring out any excess. Lie back and place one tea bag over each eye. Relax for about 10 minutes, then remove the tea bags.

cider vinegar

Made from fermented apple juice and rich in enzymes, cider vinegar has been used for centuries to aid digestion.

Apart from its beneficial action on the digestion, cider vinegar helps symptoms such as heartburn and improves metabolism. The enzymes also help to dissolve calcium deposits, making it a popular joint health aid. Cider vinegar contains cholesterol-supporting pectin, which is good for heart health, and the perfect balance of 19 minerals. It has many system-cleansing benefits, while topically it maintains healthy skin.

PROPERTIES/ACTIONS
- Aids digestion
- Rich in enzymes
- Good for arthritis
- Contains pectin
- Promotes healthy skin

PARTS USED
- Cider vinegar

OXYMEL (TRADITIONAL MEDICINAL DRINK)

apple cider vinegar
pure honey
water

Combine equal amounts of apple cider vinegar and honey in a glass jar. Shake to combine. Take 1 teaspoon with symptoms, or add eight times the amount of water to create a juice for regular sipping.

olive oil

Central to the Mediterranean diet, olive oil appears to lower the risk of heart disease, as well as treating many other complaints.

Olive oil is a monounsaturated fat that lowers levels of harmful LDL cholesterol while leaving the beneficial HDL cholesterol alone. It contains other heart-healthy compounds, as well as antioxidants. Rich in vitamin E, it also stimulates the secretion of bile, helping to soften and expel gallstones.

Olive oil was used for anointing the body in ancient Greek religious rituals.

PROPERTIES/ACTIONS
- Lowers LDL cholesterol
- Rich in vitamin E
- Stimulates secretion of bile
- Laxative

PARTS USED
- Whole ripe olives

CAPER & OLIVE OIL TAPENADE

125ml (4fl oz/½ cup) extra virgin olive oil
5 tbsp capers
80g (2¾oz/½ cup) pitted green olives
2 flat anchovy fillets
4 garlic cloves

Blend the ingredients in a food processor. Serve with bread.

097

brewer's yeast

PROPERTIES/ACTIONS
- Treats fatigue
- Boosts immunity
- Heals the skin

PARTS USED
- Dried brewer's yeast

Containing almost 50 percent protein, lecithin and unrivalled levels of B-complex vitamins, together with valuable minerals, brewer's yeast has long been used for its medicinal properties.

Brewer's yeast is a valuable remedy for fatigue and stress-related symptoms. It is rich in the nucleic acid RNA, as well as zinc, which are both vital to the immune system. Used topically in a compress, brewer's yeast is healing for skin complaints. Holding up to 70 percent moisture, it is excellent for regenerating healthy tissue.

BREWER'S YEAST COMPRESS *for skin complaints*

225g (8oz/1 cup) powdered brewer's yeast
warm water
cotton cloth
small blanket

Combine the brewer's yeast with warm water to make a soft, moist paste (about the consistency of mustard). Spread onto the cotton cloth and apply to the affected area. Cover with the blanket and leave in place until the paste begins to dry. Remove, flush the area with cold water and allow to dry. Repeat according to symptoms.

black strap molasses

Dark, sticky and rich in flavour, black strap molasses is an old-fashioned natural sweetener with high levels of nutrients.

Black strap molasses is rich in iron and is a fantastic remedy for rebuilding the blood and fighting against anaemia and fatigue. It also contains calcium, copper, manganese, potassium and magnesium, which help to prevent osteoporosis, promote a healthy nervous system and muscles, and boost immunity. According to Chinese medicine black strap molasses moistens the lungs and treats dry coughs.

PROPERTIES/ACTIONS
- Rich in nutrients
- Treats anaemia
- Helps prevent osteoporosis

PARTS USED
- Molasses from sugar cane

BLACK STRAP MOLASSES BARBECUE SAUCE

125g (4½oz/½ cup) black strap molasses
250ml (9fl oz/2 cups) tomato sauce
125ml (4fl oz/½ cup) balsamic vinegar
juice of 2 medium lemons
85g (3oz/½ cup) brown sugar
cayenne pepper, to taste

Combine the ingredients in a heat-proof bowl. Place over a saucepan of boiling water, stirring occasionally, until reduced by a third. Remove from the heat and allow the sauce to thicken as it cools.

honey

- Helps insomnia
- Treats fungal infections
- Aids healing

PARTS USED
- Bees' honey

HONEY DRESSING
for wounds

honey
gauze bandage

Spread some honey onto a
gauze bandage and apply it
to the wound. The amount of
honey used depends on the
amount of fluid exuding from
the wound. Large amounts of
exudate require substantial
amounts of honey. Reapply the
dressing as necessary.

Ancient societies around the world used honey
as an energy food. It has evolved as a unique and
powerful remedy for a wide variety of complaints.

So prized was the food of bees that the Romans used it instead
of gold to pay their taxes. Today, honey has become known as
"liquid gold" with nutritive and healing properties.

Composed of 38 percent fructose, 31 percent glucose, 1
percent sucrose and 9 percent other sugars, honey is the only
natural sweetener that requires no additional refining or
processing. It helps with any tendency towards hypoglycaemia
that may contribute towards insomnia and mood swings. It
also provides many nutritional substances, including vitamin
B6, thiamin, riboflavin, pantothenic acid, and trace amounts of
minerals such as calcium, copper, iron, magnesium,
manganese, phosphorus, potassium, sodium and zinc.

Honey is a recognized antioxidant and a powerful, broad-
spectrum antibiotic with both anti-fungal and anti-microbial
properties, acting against organisms that create the
Staphylococcus virus and candida infections. Honey also
contains an amazing substance called propolis, which is a
natural antibacterial that helps to prevent and treat coughs and
colds, as well as stomach disorders. The antibacterial content

found in Manuka honey of New Zealand has been shown to kill the *Helicobacter pylori* bug that causes stomach ulcers, while unfiltered honey contains pollen grains and helps hayfever.

Used topically, honey has a powerful antiseptic effect for the treatment of ulcers, burns and wounds. It has an anti-inflammatory action, reducing swelling and pain, and by stimulating the regrowth of tissue under the skin's surface, honey helps the healing mechanism.

In ancient Greece the alcoholic honey drink mead was regarded as the drink of the gods.

rock salt

Since the beginning of Greek medicine, salt has commonly been used as an inhalant for respiratory diseases, and topically for the skin.

PROPERTIES/ACTIONS
- Expectorant
- Treats respiratory troubles
- Good for sore throats
- Builds immunity
- Conditions the skin

PARTS USED
- Rock salt crystals

Salt has expectant powers and may relieve coughs, colds and sinusitis. The inhalation of steam from salt water has anti-inflammatory effects, offering further relief from respiratory symptoms, and salt can be used as a sore-throat gargle. Salt baths increase circulation and the elimination of toxins. They may condition the skin, relieve eczema, treat tired muscles and build up resistance to disease.

The ancient Greeks first noted that eating salty food promoted basic body health.

SALT-WATER NASAL WASH *for nasal symptoms*

250ml (l9fl oz/1 cup) warm water
pinch of salt
pinch of turmeric, optional

Mix together the ingredients and pour into a small jug with a narrow spout. Inhale the salty mixture (through the narrow spout) up one nostril. Tilt your head back and allow the mixture to drain into the back of your mouth before spitting it out, then do the same with the other nostril. Repeat up to five times a day with symptoms.

ailments directory

ANAEMIA

Anaemia occurs when the body is unable to produce enough red blood cells and therefore haemoglobin. Foods rich in iron can help.

Foods/herbs to use

apricot (p.12); beef (p.102); beetroot (p.27); black bean (p.47); black strap molasses (p.117); broccoli (p.37); chicory (p.85); lamb (p.103); lentil (p.43); nettle (p.82); quinoa (p.56); rye (p.57); spinach (p.24); strawberry (p.17); wheatgrass (p.100)

ARTHRITIS (RHEUMATOID)

Antioxidant-rich fruits and vegetables, as well as nuts, seeds and oily fish may help this imflammatory condition, which affects the joints.

Foods/herbs to use

anise (p.96); apple (p.19); artichoke (p.32); asparagus (p.31); black cohosh (p.76); cabbage (p.36); cayenne pepper (p.95); chickweed (p.88); chilli (p.42); cider vinegar (p.114); elderflower (p.80); fennel (p.64); flaxseed (p.52); horseradish (p.79); liquorice (p.63); millet (p.62); nutmeg (p.97); papaya (p.23); pineapple (p.14); salmon (p.104); St John's wort (p.84); strawberry (p.17); turmeric (p.94)

ASTHMA

Asthma sufferers experience inflamed air passages of the lungs. This can cause extra-sensitivity to "triggers" or allergens including milk, wheat, nuts and fish, which may be best avoided.

Foods/herbs to use

black cohosh (p.76); cayenne pepper (p.95); coffee (p.112); elderflower (p.80); garlic (p.73); liquorice (p.63); onion (p.41); sweet potato (p.34); thyme (p.81)

BRONCHITIS

Mucus-creating dairy products are best avoided in this viral infection of the lining of the bronchial tubes.

Foods/herbs to use

aduki bean (p.46); anise (p.96); apricot (p.12); black cohosh

(p.76); chilli (p.42); echinacea (p.65); elderflower (p.80); flaxseed (p.52); garlic (p.73); ginger (p.92); horseradish (p.79); lavender (p.86); lemon (p.10); onion (p.41); sage (p.68); sunflower seed (p.51); sweet potato (p.34); thyme (p.81); watercress (p.40)

COMMON COLD
Avoiding dairy products and eating fruits and vegetables can help fight the virus.
Foods/herbs to use
blueberry (p.21); chilli (p.42); cinnamon (p.91); cranberry (p.20); echinacea (p.65); elderflower (p.80); eucalyptus (p.70); garlic (p.73); ginger (p.92); grapefruit (p.18); honey (p.118); lemon (p.10); orange (p.11); peppermint (p.67); prawn (p.105); rock salt (p.120);

rosemary (p.66); sage (p.68); tea tree (p.89); thyme (p.81)

DIABETES
When the pancreas cannot produce enough insulin or the body becomes resistant to insulin, diabetes occurs.
Foods/herbs to use
aloe vera (p.71); apple (p.19); artichoke (p.32); carrot (p.35); oats (p.60); potato (p.28); sweet potato (p.34)

ECZEMA
Eczema is an inflammatory skin condition that can be caused by a food sensitivity. Identify and avoid any common allergens. A diet rich in essential fatty acids, vitamin A and zinc can help.
Foods/herbs to use
avocado (p.26); brewer's yeast

(p.116); carrot (p.35); cayenne pepper (p.95); chamomile (p.87); chickweed (p.88); comfrey (p.74); flaxseed (p.52); lavender (p.88); nutmeg (p.97); oats (p.60); papaya (p.23); pumpkin seed (p.50); quinoa (p.56); rock salt (p.120); rosemary (p.66); salmon (p.104); sunflower seed (p.51); turmeric (p.94); wheatgrass (p.100)

FUNGAL INFECTIONS
Food is a common cause of fungal infections. Avoid alcohol, dairy and refined sugar products, and limit yeast consumption.
Foods/herbs to use
garlic (p.73); ginger (p.92); grapefruit (p.18); honey (p.118); lavender (p.86); millet (p.62); rice (p.55); tea tree (p.89); thyme (p.81)

INDIGESTION

Indigestion involves discomfort in the digestive tract. Some acid-forming foods, such as citrus fruits and red meat, can cause it, while others help to prevent or ease it.

Foods/herbs to use

artichoke (p.32); banana (p.22); carrot (p.35); cayenne pepper (p.95); cider vinegar (p.114); cinnamon (p.91); fennel (p.64); garlic (p.73); ginger (p.92); grapefruit (p.18); hawthorn (p.83); lemon balm (p.90); liquorice (p.63); millet (p.62); papaya (p.23); peppermint (p.67); rice (p.55); slippery elm (p.77)

INFLUENZA (FLU)

Flu is a viral infection with extreme cold-like symptoms.
Use foods and herbs that help to boost immunity.

Foods/herbs to use

see common cold

INSOMNIA

Insomnia can be caused by many things, among them stimulants such as caffeine, which is best avoided. Foods that treat the liver, as well as calming, soothing herbs, can help.

Foods/herbs to use

apricot (p.12); chamomile (p.87); honey (p.118); lemon balm (p.90); nutmeg (p.97); oats (p.60); oyster (p.106)

IRRITABLE BOWEL SYNDROME (IBS)

Symptoms include abdominal bloating and pain, constipation and/or
diarrhoea, and poor nutrient absorption. Causes can include food allergens.

Foods/herbs to use

anise (p.96); asparagus (p.31); chamomile (p.87); dandelion (p.69); fennel (p.64); horseradish (p.79); oats (p.60); rice (p.55); rosemary (p.66); slippery elm (p.77)

SINUSITIS

Due to inflammation in the nasal passages, sinusitis causes symptoms including headache and a blocked nose. Avoid any allergens, eat foods with anti-inflammatory properties and use herbs to help boost immunity.

Foods/herbs to use

See common cold, horseradish (p.79); pineapple (p.14)

URINARY TRACT INFECTIONS

Infections of the kidneys, bladder and urethra occur when microorganisms remain in the urinary tract and begin to multiply.

Foods/herbs to use

aduki bean (p.46); barley (p.59); blueberry (p.21); celery (p.30); chickpea (p.48); chicory (p.85); cranberry (p.20); fennel (p.64); quinoa (p.56); St John's wort (p.84)

MIGRAINE

This causes severe headaches as well as other symptoms such as sensitivity to light, nausea and vomiting. Potential food allergens should be avoided.

Foods/herbs to use

feverfew (p.78); coffee can help in some cases (p.112)

STRESS

The effects of stress release adrenaline in the body; in excessive amounts, this can be detrimental to health. Symptoms range from anxiety and headaches, to exhaustion and other more severe complications.

Foods/herbs to use

aduki bean (p.46); apricot (p.12); barley (p.59); brewer's yeast (p.116); chamomile (p.87); ginseng (p.72); hawthorn (p.83); lemon balm (p.90); soya bean (p.44); sunflower seed (p.51); thyme (p.81)

FLUID RETENTION

A number of natural remedies may help to relieve fluid retention.

Foods/herbs to use

aduki bean (p.46); chicken (p.108); chickpea (p.48); dandelion (p.69); fennel (p.64)

HEADACHE

Headaches can occur as a result of irregular meals, a noisy or stuffy environment, excitement, or certain foods, such as cheese, chocolate and red wine.

Foods/herbs to use

cayenne pepper (p.95); lavender (p.86); liquorice (p.63); peppermint (p.67); rosemary (p.66); rye (p.57); seaweed (p.99)

PREMENSTRUAL SYNDROME (PMS)

This occurs in some women and may involve irritability, tension, depression, fatigue, fluid retention, backache and abdominal pain. Relaxation

and avoidance of certain foods, such as salt, caffeine and chocolate, may help.

Foods/herbs to use

black bean (p.47); black cohosh (p.76); chamomile (p.87); chicken (p.108); feverfew (p.78); flaxseed (p.52); lemon balm (p.90); millet (p.62); nettle (p.82); oyster (p.106); rosemary (p.66); seaweed (p.99); turmeric (p.94)

WOUNDS

Damage to the skin and underlying tissue that has been caused by injury may be relieved by remedies such as poultices applied directly to the skin.

Foods/herbs to use

aloe vera (p.71); buckwheat (p.58); honey (p.118); lavender (p.86); lemon (p.10); lemon balm (p.90); slippery elm (p.77); tea tree (p.89); thyme (p.81); wheatgrass (p.100)

HAYFEVER

Caused by allergens such as plant pollen, house dust mites, or certain foods, such as milk, eggs, shellfish, nuts and dried fruits, hayfever is best treated by the avoidance of the relevant allergen. Certain foods and herbs may help alleviate the condition.

Foods/herbs to use

avocado (p.26); beetroot (p.27); elderflower (p.80); honey (p.118); nettle (p.82); papaya (p.23)

CONSTIPATION

The most common cause of constipation is insufficient fibre in the diet. Foods containing plenty of fibre, such as fruits and vegetables as well as wholemeal bread and other products, can help to prevent and ease it.

Foods/herbs to use

aloe vera (p.71); apple (p.19); banana (p.22); beetroot (p.27); coffee (p.112); dandelion (p.69); fig (p.13); flaxseed (p.52); liquorice (p.63); olive oil (p.115); papaya (p.23); rye (p.57); soya bean (p.44); spinach (p.24)

INSECT BITES

Wash the area of the insect bite with soap and water, then apply a cold compress to it.

Foods/herbs to use

coffee (p.112); eucalyptus (p.70); onion (p.41)

CANCER

This condition is due to the unrestrained growth of cells in body organs or tissues. The symptoms of cancer may be alleviated by certain foods and herbs, and there is evidence that some food types could have a preventative effect on the development of cancer.

Foods/herbs to use

almond (p.49); beef (p.102); Brazil nut (p.54); cabbage (p.36); carrot (p.35); cauliflower (p.25); cranberry (p.20); flaxseed (p.52); mushroom (p.38); olive oil (p.115); onion (p.41); potato (p.28); prawn (p.105); rye (p.57); salmon (p.104); spinach (p.24); sprouts (p.98); sweet potato (p.34); tea tree (p.89); tomato (p.39); turmeric (p.94); yoghurt (p.110)

DEPRESSION

Psychotherapy and drugs are often used to treat depression, and certain natural remedies may help the condition.

Foods/herbs to use

avocado (p.26); Brazil nut (p.54); buckwheat (p.58); coffee (p.112); milk (p.109); oats (p.60); raspberry (p.16); rice (p.55); St John's wort (p.84); sunflower seed (p.51)

FATIGUE

Lethargy is a common symptom of many disorders. Energy-providing foods are useful in boosting energy.

Foods/herbs to use

artichoke (p.32); avocado (p.26); barley (p.59); black strap molasses (p.117); brewer's yeast (p.116); ginseng (p.72); honey

(p.118); lamb (p.103); oats (p.60); orange (p.11); oyster (p.106); pumpkin seed (p.50); raspberry (p.16); rice (p.55); rosemary (p.66); soya bean (p.44); spinach (p.24); St John's wort (p.84); wheatgrass (p.100)

OSTEOPOROSIS

Involving loss of protein matrix from the bones, osteoporosis causes bones to become brittle. Eating foods rich in calcium can help to prevent it.

Foods/herbs to use

beef (p.102); black strap molasses (p.117); broccoli (p.37); milk (p.109); millet (p.62); nettle (p.82); oats (p.60); oyster (p.106); pineapple (p.14); prawn (p.105); rye (p.57); soya bean (p.44); yoghurt (p.110)

glossary

Allontoin an anti-inflammatory stimulating cell regeneration.

Analgesic used to relieve pain.

Antioxidant compound that inhibits the effects of free radicals, found in fruits and vegetables.

Arginine organic compound found in animal proteins.

Asparagine detoxifying amino acid.

Astringent draws together, constricts, binds.

***Bifida* bacteria** beneficial bacteria that inhabit the intestinal tract and help fight off infection.

Bromelain anti-inflammatory enzyme that helps digest proteins.

Capsaicin active component of chilli peppers.

Carminative removes gases from the gastrointestinal tract.

Conjugated linoleic acid (CLA) naturally occurring fatty acid.

Curcumin detoxifying, anti-inflammatory pigment found in turmeric.

Cynarin detoxifying, liver-supporting substance.

Demulcent soothes and softens when applied locally.

Diuretic increases the secretion of urine.

E. coli abbreviation of a term for intestinal bacteria.

Emollient softens and soothes the skin when applied locally.

Essential fatty acids good fats including linoleic acid, omega-3 fatty acids and monounsaturated fats, which cannot be made in the body but must come from the diet.

Expectorant facilitates the removal of the secretions of the pulmonary mucous membranes.

Flavonoid umbrella term for anti-inflammatory bioactive compounds.

Free radicals highly reactive molecules that can destroy tissues.

Fructooligosaccharide natural fibre that exists in unprocessed fruits and vegetables.

Gingerol source of spiciness in ginger.

Glycyrrhizic acid anti-inflammatory agent.

Helicobacter pylori bacterium that causes chronic inflammation of the inner lining of the stomach.

Indole aromatic, organic compound.

Isoflavones compounds that mimic the action of oestrogen.

Lactobacillus bacterium that converts lactose and other simple sugars to lactic acid.

Lactose sugar in milk, needing lactasein enzyme to digest.

Laxative stimulates the action of the intestines to eliminate waste from the body.

Lecithin dry powder source of phospholipids high in B-fatty acids.

Lycopene antioxidant carotenoid found in red foods.

Malic acid acid found in apples.

Mucilage thick, glutinous substance, related to natural gums.

Nervine acts as a nerve sedative.

Phytonutrient plant compound with health-giving properties.

Plant lignans naturally occurring plant chemicals.

Polyphenols compounds used for chemical synthesis

Prebiotic non-digestible fibres that are the energy source for beneficial bacteria in the colon.

Prostaglandins compounds synthesized from fatty acids, produced as needed by cell membranes in most body tissues.

Protease enzyme that cuts another protein.

Quercetin anti-inflammatory flavonoid found in onions.

Staphylococcus a type of parasitic bacterium.

Sterols fats bound to plant fibres, with protective agents.

index

ACKNOWLEDGEMENTS
The author would like to thank her husband Josh for his encouragement and patience, her two children Louis and Olivia for being such a joyful source of inspiration, and her parents Derek and Carole for their ongoing support.

The publishers thank Peter Jarrett of the Medicinal Herb Garden at Middlesex University, England, for denoting herbal samples, and Beatriz Linhares for providing and preparing herb samples for photography.